"There are many books that provide insight on the college admissions process, but none is specifically geared toward Black families. There are things that Black families should know as they go through the college search and selection process, and this book provides direction and clear answers."

—JAWAAN J. WALLACE, Director of Enrollment Management & Collegiate Partnerships, Marlborough School

"A unique, refreshing, and much-needed resource from two admissions insiders. This book is a tremendously valuable guide for Black students and their families as they seek to make informed decisions, ask astute questions, and ultimately select the best college for them."

—RICK CLARK, Assistant Vice Provost / Executive Director of Undergraduate Admission, Georgia Institute of Technology; coauthor of *The Truth about College Admission*

"I appreciate that Fields and Herndon-Brown consider the intersection of race and the value of the HBCU. This book is a must-read for Black students and their families. I now feel more prepared for my own three children to begin the process."

—ERIN ROSE, parent and Florida A&M University graduate

"I am confident *The Black Family's Guide to College Admissions* will become a valuable resource for counselors, mentors, and others who are a sounding board of reason in the lives of graduating seniors and their families, especially for first-generation college-goers, who will need to create realistic options for themselves."

—L. M. ROZIERS, President, Mitch22 Foundation, Inc.

THE
Black Family's
Guide to
College
Admissions

A CONVERSATION ABOUT
EDUCATION, PARENTING, AND RACE

SECOND EDITION

TIMOTHY L. FIELDS AND
SHEREEM HERNDON-BROWN

Foreword by Akil Bello

JOHNS HOPKINS UNIVERSITY PRESS
Baltimore

© 2022, 2024 Johns Hopkins University Press
All rights reserved. Published 2024
Printed in the United States of America on acid-free paper
9 8 7 6 5 4 3 2 1

Johns Hopkins University Press
2715 North Charles Street
Baltimore, Maryland 21218
www.press.jhu.edu

Library of Congress Cataloging-in-Publication Data

Names: Fields, Timothy L., 1976– author. | Herndon-Brown, Shereem, 1974–
  author.
Title: The Black family's guide to college admissions : a conversation
  about education, parenting, and race / Timothy L. Fields and Shereem
  Herndon-Brown ; Foreword by Akil Bello.
Description: Second edition. | Baltimore, Maryland : Johns Hopkins
  University Press, 2024. | Includes bibliographical references and index.
Identifiers: LCCN 2023038032 | ISBN 9781421448961 (paperback) | ISBN
  9781421448978 (ebook)
Subjects: LCSH: African Americans—Education (Higher) | African American
  universities and colleges. | Universities and colleges—United
  States—Admission. | College applications—United States. | Education,
  Higher—Parent participation.
Classification: LCC LC2781 .F54 2024 | DDC
  378.73089/96073—dc23/eng/20230816
LC record available at https://lccn.loc.gov/2023038032

A catalog record for this book is available from the British Library.

*Special discounts are available for bulk purchases of this book. For more information,
please contact Special Sales at specialsales@jh.edu.*

I dedicate this book to Regent Elridge McMillan and his lifelong dedication to promoting educational access and equality and to the lives of Ramone Harper, Noah Johnson, and Myron Burney, who were living testaments that success has more than one path! #TB4L

TLF

To all my former students at Brooklyn Friends School, Westtown School, Riverdale Country School, and Trinity School—I wrote this for you. When you got into your top-choice colleges, I celebrated, and when you didn't, I blamed myself. I could have and should have done more. You drive me to serve my SAA teammates, students, charter schools, and educators with brutal honesty and relentless effort.

To my children—Sydney, Kerry, Sai, and Samara. My only wish is that you make a contribution to this world as I am trying to do, in your way, and with your style. Just promise me that you'll celebrate being young, gifted, and Black.

To my wife, Keri—Howard. 1911. 1999. 4ever$.

SHB

Contents

Part I. Context

Part II. X Factors

Part III. Process

CONTENTS

Foreword

Akil Bello

Prior to 2022 I did not know Shereem or Tim. One day Shereem called me, a stranger, to discuss "something important." It turned out that he and Tim, his coauthor, were putting on a virtual event whose title shared some words with the name of an event I was doing with the College Board. He wanted to make sure I didn't think they were encroaching on my turf. I was amused, honored, and surprised.

This stranger had called because he cared about my perception of his actions. This stranger was thoughtful enough to consider whether his words might cause problems for others. He had taken the time to get my contact information from a mutual friend, reach out to me, and explain the situation so that I didn't misinterpret their ordering of a few words. I was impressed by the brotherhood I felt he was showing and became curious about his work.

This phone call taught me all I needed to know about Shereem and what I would come to know about Tim: they care. About education, college admissions, students and families, and the complexity of the application process. After I read the first edition of *The Black Family's Guide to College Admissions: A Conversation about Education, Parenting, and Race*, my respect for them only grew, and it's why I was excited to write this foreword for the book's second edition. They had taken the time. They had worked hard to get it right. And they did not want to do this work alone.

The Black Family's Guide to Admissions is the book I've thought about writing for years. It's a book that's been missing from the college admissions literature. It's one designed to help families and educators navigate the landscape of options in American higher education from a *Black* perspective, with all the variety, nuance, and complexity that perspective brings. Having worked around college admission and access for thirty years, I know intimately how challenging it is for Black families, regardless of wealth or opportunity, to undertake the process of finding, applying to, and comparing offers from colleges. There are cultural, historical, financial, and social issues that must be weighed at every stage and in every decision we make. Just as important as it is for parents, Tim and Shereem's book is a resource too for educators and allies, who may not be Black but who want to better understand and support Black students and their families as they plan for college.

Go into a bookstore, or do a Google search more likely, and you'll find plenty of books that purport to guide families on how to research colleges, improve an applicant's chances for admission, and pay for college. But few of these books discuss the needs, wants, and perspectives of Black families. And even fewer still capture the nuance of that discussion. The books you'll find are often full of data but lack wisdom, are often full of advice but lack the weight of experience that grants credibility to their advice.

Tim and Shereem have brought their combined decades of experience in college admissions and counseling, together with their many years of being Black parents, in providing readers with a perspective not available in other books. They thoughtfully discuss a range of educational experiences for Black students (the experiences we've had and the experiences we want for our children). They have a lot to say about applying to selective schools, and that's because admission to these schools tends not to be simple or straightforward, not because the authors presume that selective schools are the only ones worth considering. Their book provides a clear-eyed look at all the necessary legwork, from identifying schools to prepping for standardized tests to making financial plans, that a family has to do if they want their child to compete in the application pool of selective institutions.

And no discussion of a Black family's college search would be complete without taking an unflinching look at the perceptions and realities of Historically Black Colleges and Universities. Most college admissions books either ignore HBCUs or focus on them solely. Tim and Shereem take a different approach: they explore the tensions that can arise in families when comparing the merits of HBCUs with those of predominantly white institutions: education versus brand, cost versus value, career planning versus personal growth.

I read *The Black Family's Guide to College Admissions* while my eldest son was working his way through the fall of eleventh grade as the leading scorer of his basketball team, I'm proud to say. I related to the advice Shereem offers about the lure and value of athletics. When I read about Tim's experience at an HBCU, I felt FOMO (or "fear of missing out," in the shorthand of social media) because I had transferred from an HBCU (University of the Virgin Islands) to two PWIs (St. John's University and Pratt Institute). Tim's experience steeled my resolve to include HBCUs on my children's college lists. As an education professional, I appreciate the way they handle being torn between selecting colleges for their brand recognition or for the quality of the educational experience. Their consistent highlighting of schools other than those that typically get the most attention is not only rare for an admissions guidebook but also hugely important.

Tim and Shereem encourage us to think about the costs, cultural and financial, of going to a PWI versus an HBCU. They explore myths of feeling pressured to attend the "right" college. The notion that only a small set of elite schools can lead graduates to success is wrong; instead, they encourage nuanced exploration of the decision-making that goes into a *college choosing a student* versus *a family choosing a college*. They don't shy away from toppling one of the shakiest beliefs about admissions today, stating clearly and unequivocally that despite what critics of affirmative action want the public to believe, being Black is not (and has never been) enough for an applicant to gain admission. When it comes to admissions, an institution's priorities matter and family choices matter, and what matters most is finding the right overlap between institutional priorities and family needs.

Much of my work these days focuses on myth-busting around the elitism associated with college admissions and the hyper-focus on admission to the exclusion of considering what happens after a student is accepted. I spend a lot of time explaining that being famous or wealthy does equate with being good and that a college rejecting more students than it admits does not indicate its quality. In forty-four articles of higher education reporting published by the *New York Times*, from January 2020 to July 2022, one highly rejective college (out of the 2,300-plus four-year colleges in America) was mentioned fourteen times and another mentioned five times, while no other college got more than three mentions. It's important for families to pay attention to and resist the lure of reductive assessments like rankings and "best of" lists that are common clickbait on the internet. This book takes great pains to highlight an array of colleges dedicated to helping students learn what they need in order to succeed in life.

Tim and Shereem urge us to start thinking about the college admissions process much earlier than a student's senior year in high school. Families should consider how decisions made about a child's education in elementary and middle school can later impact their chances in college admissions. They provide tools and tables that show us how to make decisions about a child's education that are better informed by data. They pose questions that all parents should be asking:

- What should my family look for in a college?
- What should my child expect from a college education?
- How do I figure out what colleges are "good"?
- What can I do to prepare my child for life after high school?

All parents, Black and non-Black, can find something of value in this book. It accomplishes what many others don't in that it manages to be succinct yet rich in evaluating the complexity of applying to selective colleges. Whether recommending what questions to ask or how to arrive at satisfying answers to them, the authors help us think through the process of being a *family* considering educational opportunities together. Their parenting advice such as "I will no longer allow my child to navigate adult situations alone" will stick with me beyond my son's experience with college admissions.

This book is exactly what it claims to be: a book written by two Black parents who are highly informed about the college admissions process for other Black parents who are less informed about it. Perhaps foremost among its benefits, this book will encourage families to engage in intense reflection on their values, resources, and objectives in applying to college. Written in an easy to understand and thoughtful way, it sets in motion many conversations about the goals and purposes of educational attainment that will continue past its pages.

Even after thirty years in the industry, I found myself questioning and learning as I read the book. And that, I think, is the point.

Akil Bello is a nationally recognized advocate for educational policy and an expert on standardized testing. He writes about education in a blog on his website Bellowings at https://akilbello.com.

Preface

When we set out to write *The Black Family's Guide to College Admissions*, we had one primary purpose in mind: to provide information and insight into the college admissions process, specifically as it relates to the lived experience of Black Americans. What we found, though, as we toured the country and gave virtual programs following its publication is that Black families have so many questions to answer when they think about college admissions. Beyond *How do I apply to college?*, there's *Why should I go college?*, *How can we pay for it?*, *How is my child going to be judged based on their particular academic profile?*, and many others. Talking to families drove home to us the importance of protecting mental health during the college admissions process.

In 2020 the big topic was "test optional" admissions and what that meant for students. This is still an important consideration, but it shrinks next to what the Supreme Court's ruling on race-conscious admissions means for Black families. In summer 2023 the court ruled that race can no longer be considered in the review of college applications. Add to this the rise of ChatGPT, an application that uses artificial intelligence, which has big implications for writing application essays that we are only beginning to appreciate. With these important changes upon us, we knew we had to update our book with a second edition to better inform students, families, and educators on what has become our mantra: *redefine success in the college admissions process.*

We must remind ourselves and our children that money does not equal success. What's more, most people in this country, regardless of race, achieve their goals in life without ever going to an Ivy League school or to any college or university ranked highly by *U.S. News and World Report*. In fact, many individuals have changed, and will change, the world for the better without going to college at all. When you think of the most famous Black people in our country who attended college, they graduated from all kinds of schools.

Of course, we think of President Barack Obama and First Lady Michelle Obama, who graduated from Columbia University and Princeton University, respectively. Both are successful and both attended PWIs (short for predominantly white institutions). But make no mistake, their time in the Oval Office may never have come to fruition if not for the endorsement of Oprah Winfrey, a graduate of Tennessee State University, an HBCU, or Historically Black College and University. Kamala Harris, now vice president, is a proud graduate of Howard University, an HBCU. So, yes, success can come to those who attend an HBCU, just as it can follow an education from a PWI. In the book's first edition, we highlighted the colleges and universities attended by many prominent Black college graduates; in the second edition, we have included even more. We are adamant in believing that your child's success in life does not depend on which type of institution they attend.

Many students and parents associate "dream school" with the Ivy League or another school of that ilk, but we want students, families, and educators to appreciate the far wider range of options available to them. There are over four thousand colleges and universities in the United States, and two thousand of them offer four-year bachelor's degrees. Despite this abundance of higher education options, most public attention is directed at only fifty to one hundred of these institutions. In consequence, many outstanding institutions get overlooked, and unfairly so, we say.

There is nothing wrong with aspiring to a selective institution, but when a child can only visualize themselves at one dream school, they often are setting themselves up for disappointment. Getting into a selective school is hard to do, and rejection by one often seems unfair from an applicant's point of view. Yes, your student may have worked hard in high school, but so have many other students. You will never fully understand the institutional priorities behind a school's admission criteria or enrollment management methods. You'll have to accept rejection without knowing, with certainty, why. This reality can lead to emotional distress. We, as educators, as parents, as concerned Black men, implore you, parents, to help your child redefine what success means to them.

We know from experience, in our personal and professional lives, that success is not predicated on going to a particular college or university. We are sure that you too know people from your personal and professional networks whom you admire who did not attend a top-tier institution. Keep that knowledge active in your mind when undertaking the college admissions process with your child. Life is about being intelligent, engaged, compassionate, and committed to your purpose. The college admissions process is complicated enough already, given all the variables that students and families must consider—where they attend secondary school, what classes they take there, what activities bring them joy and let them excel, and whether they take the SAT or the ACT. No one formula can guarantee acceptance or postgraduate success. Parents, don't further complicate this process by limiting your child's college choices to places that admit less than 20 percent of the students that apply. Most colleges and universities, by contrast, accept over 60 percent of applicants. We need to see these schools as places where our children can thrive and where we can be proud to send them. Let's keep an open mind and define success on our terms, not simply according to the brand name of an institution.

As we reflect on the word *success*, let us recall a beautiful January day in 2021 in Washington, DC, when a crowd gathered for the inauguration of Joseph R. Biden as the forty-sixth president of the United States. On the dais for this momentous occasion were members of Congress, celebrities, and family members of the elected officials. We viewers watched a transfer of executive power witnessed in person by notable Black people in attendance, including the first female vice president of the United States, Kamala Harris, who identifies as Black and Southeast Asian. Vice President Harris's alma mater, Howard University, is the same school attended years before by Thurgood Marshall, a US Supreme Court justice; it is located less than three miles from the Capitol steps where Harris was sworn in.

We have mentioned already the former president and first lady, who were also in attendance that day. In the crowd as well was Congressman Jim Clyburn, a major catalyst in the election of the new president, who had donned his South Carolina State University baseball cap to show his great pride in his home state and his HBCU alma mater. A highlight of the day was no doubt the powerful poem delivered by Amanda Gorman, national youth poet laureate, who attended Harvard College. There were many others in attendance that day, but we highlight these individuals because of the different educational choices they made.

These individuals are, by any measure, successful, regardless of what institution awarded their degree. The goal of any parent should be for their child to live a healthy life, be a good citizen, and ultimately become successful, however they may choose to define that for themselves. As for Barack Obama, Michelle Obama, Kamala Harris, Jim Clyburn, and Amanda Gorman, each had different opportunities and life circumstances that may have influenced where they went to college. Despite differences, though, in resources, size, location, and institutional type, each of the schools they attended offered something that helped them find success. Did they know when they chose their school—with the help of a parent, college counselor, or family friend perhaps—that they would later take part in American history that day? Likely not, but the fact they attended such different universities says a lot about the unique higher education system we have in this country, which offers so many opportunities to students looking for a college education.

Their choice of where to go to college did not determine their presence at the inauguration; rather, the key was what they did with the opportunities afforded to them both in college and beyond. As parents, it is essential that you and your child understand the choices that are in front of them. Whether they choose to go to college, aspire to be an artist or athlete, or have entrepreneurial courage and drive, you know your child best, and as they enter their formative years, you can probably tell the path they are on, given their abilities, talents, and other characteristics. *College is not for everyone*, and the path to and through college can be difficult. The multiple decisions that go into it, especially for Black families, have multiple layers that extend beyond simply choosing which college to apply to and attend.

How Did We Come to Write This Book?

In June of 2020, a few weeks after the tragic slaying of George Floyd, the entire country was trying to deal with both the tragedy that had occurred in Minneapolis and the reality that violent racism was still alive and thriving in America long after the end of segregation. While many wanted to view what happened to George Floyd as an isolated incident, his death was one in a long series of unarmed Black people who died at the hands of police. These deaths provided a reality check and awakening for a country that had turned a blind eye to injustices for far too long. Throughout the country, people of all backgrounds took to the streets to protest, signaling that these acts of injustice and racism could no longer be tolerated.

At the same time that millions were taking to the streets in protest, an online movement began in Atlanta and quickly spread nationally. Brave young Black people took to social media to express their anger and frustration at their affluent private schools for their blatant racism or for being complicit in microaggressions by white students and faculty. Thanks to the accelerated pace of social media, there soon were black@INSERTPRIVATESCHOOL posts from schools across the country that documented instances of racism against Black students. And it hurt us to read them.

We are both Black parents, and although we have made different choices about our children's schools, all of the six children between us have gone to predominantly white schools. We attended predominantly white high schools ourselves: public (Tim) and private

(Shereem). The feelings expressed in those Instagram posts, the fear, anger, and isolation, hit very close to home. As we read the posts of students, we knew they were giving voice to truths we had known for most of our adult lives. We also knew that we had to use our voices to amplify theirs and address one of the most common themes in the posts: college counseling.

We have known each other for almost a decade from working in the college admissions profession. One of us (Shereem) was an admissions officer at Georgetown University and has been a college counselor at two prestigious private schools. Given his experiences on both sides, secondary school and collegiate, he started his own independent consulting company to help families think about everything from course selection to testing options to which institutions to visit to writing application essays. In sum, his company guides families step-by-step through the entire application process up to the point when they decide what school the student will attend. The other (Tim) works on the college side as the senior associate dean of admissions at Emory University, where he spends the majority of time recruiting, reviewing applications, and building programming to promote access, not just at Emory, but for all students looking to attend a postsecondary education institution. Tim's experience is extensive as he has collaborated as an admissions expert with national educational organizations such as QuestBridge, the Jack Kent Cooke Foundation, the United Negro College Fund, and the National Merit Scholarship Corporation, in addition to having worked closely with several Federal TRiO Programs for many years.

We became friends and supported each other's writing and professional efforts. We learned that we had contrasting educational backgrounds. Shereem attended boarding school and Wesleyan University (a PWI), and Tim attended public school and Morehouse College (an HBCU). Shereem is a first-generation college graduate whose parents were both blue-collar workers, and Tim is a fourth-generation college graduate whose parents have higher education administration experience. We found it interesting that our radically different educational experiences had brought us to a similar place.

Given the racial reckoning that was happening around us, we had the momentum and motive to write something that would address the inequities we see in our personal and professional experiences in college admissions. These inequities were the subjects of so many black@INSERTPRIVATESCHOOL posts. Black students at private schools were consistently mentioning the many racial disparities in college counseling that white and Black students received. While every school may be different, the college counseling process and the guidance given to students should be the same:

- Choose appropriate classes and do well in them.
- Take standardized tests (SAT and ACT).
- Get involved in the community through activities in the arts, athletics, or volunteerism.
- Get a balanced college list from your school counselor that matches your strengths and interests.
- Have counselor and parents meet to make sure everyone is on the same page.
- Write and revise self-reflective essays.
- Get feedback on the essays from counselor, teachers, and parents.
- Feel supported.
- And, in the end, have college options.

That seems simple, right? Well, the black@INSERTPRIVATESCHOOL posts told a different story. Here are a few posts about college counseling at some of the most prestigious private schools in the country:

"My college counselor told me I would never get into an Ivy league school. She looked at my transcript and told me I did not have enough Honors and AP courses. I had 4 but that was not enough. No one ever told me how much I needed, or I would have taken more."

> "My dad is a single father and worked a lot. He could not come
> to my college meetings. When I talked to my college counselor,
> she told me I should just apply to state schools because of
> financial aid. She never told me that many private colleges
> are need blind and may have wanted me for diversity based on
> my race and class. I felt that she dismissed me because my dad
> was not in her face."

> "When I asked my college counselor about Spelman, he told me
> that I should not go to a Black school because the world is not
> Black. I told him that all the schools he was suggesting were white
> and that the world wasn't white either. He barely spoke to me
> after that, and I only got into a few colleges and ended up trans-
> ferring later on."

As the posts surfaced, it became overwhelming for us as Black parents and college admissions professionals to read them. We knew
that what was being shared was true because, unfortunately, we had
seen and experienced it.

When I (Shereem) was a school counselor at two private schools,
the undermatching of students of color—Black and Latinx—
happened all the time. And what is *undermatching*? Undermatching
is when a school counselor poorly evaluates a student's chances for
admission. It's when they suggest colleges that are not good matches
for a student because they failed to consider the student's strengths,
interests, aspirations, culture, or family dynamics. An undermatched
college list includes only schools the counselor is familiar with or
was generated by an algorithm such as CollegeXpress or BigFuture.
Black students undermatching infuriates me. It's one thing if they
choose to apply to those schools, but when they are not presented
with all of their options, that is unacceptable given all the colleges
and universities out there. Black families who are spending money,
and perhaps sacrificing cultural acceptance, for their child to attend
a private school deserve better.

With what was happening in the United States in summer 2020, we knew that a book specifically for Black parents was needed. Yes, there are already tons of books out there about college admissions that will help with essay writing, provide procedural guidance through the standard application process, increase standardized test scores, and supply rankings and overviews of colleges. What we felt was missing from the college admissions literature, however, is a book that speaks directly to Black families and addresses issues that matter to us and have been overlooked—issues such as grappling with the idea of placing your student in a primary or secondary school where very few people will look like them, or the long-standing debate in many Black homes about the cultural and educational credibility of HBCUs compared with PWIs. Several books and organizations are specifically designed for first-generation Black college students, but we have not come across any books or programs designed for the "Black-ish" population, a reference to the ABC network show starring Tracee Ellis Ross and Anthony Anderson. By Black-ish, we mean those who went to college and are now making difficult decisions about where we live and send our children to school. We are the Black generation that has, at times, made choices that set our children up for micro- and macro-aggressions at affluent public and private schools that claim to be "allies" and "diverse."

Black-ish is a funny yet bold television show, created by Kenya Barris (Clark Atlanta University), about a Black father's determination to establish a sense of cultural identity in his family while living in a predominantly white and affluent environment. Starring Anthony Anderson (Howard University) and Tracee Ellis Ross (Brown University).

We initially thought we were writing this book just for the many Black families who might otherwise feel uninformed or overlooked in the college admissions process. However, we found out through our conversations with college counselors, many of whom were not Black, that this book was also needed to educate school counselors, college advisors, and others who are looking for insight and resources to further the goal of having more diversity, equity, and inclusion in higher education. The search for the right college is personal, but for Black families, given the racial history of this country and the exclusionary foundation of the educational system, some additional issues must be considered. We want to bring these issues to the forefront and provide context for them. Conversations about these issues have been going on for years in small circles, but they need amplification and a bigger platform.

From the start we wanted this book to showcase the love we have for our culture and our children. This book is intended for Black parents like us who strive to do what's best for our children, having perhaps more resources available to us than what we were raised with. Many of us struggle to know what the "best" education looks like for our Black children when we want them to be secure in their culture and identity but also want them to get a quality education. Our aim is to explain how college admissions works and what Black parents need to think about as they puzzle through how to educate their children at the best schools possible. The conversations these decisions require are not easy for families to have because many Black college graduates believe their children should attend the same kind of institution they did. Some of us who went to PWIs—especially in the Northeast—are curious about HBCUs, but since attending an HBCU wasn't our experience, we might turn to the rankings in *U.S. News and World Report*. In our own two households we have graduates from both PWIs and HBCUs. We have already mentioned our alma maters: Tim (HBCU) and Shereem (PWI). Relevant too are those of our spouses: Shereem's wife (Howard University, an HBCU) and Tim's wife (University of Miami, a PWI).

Yes, we are college admissions experts who have spent thousands of hours working with families to help them navigate the college admissions process, but we are parents first. We know firsthand that this discussion about what is the best college for our children is complicated and needs to start earlier. We do not claim to have all the answers, but we do know that we have a lot of information. Black students and families deserve better, and we hope to offer what we know to help anyone who will listen. We no longer want to talk only among ourselves. Instead, we want to grow a community by encouraging these conversations about Black families and our educational choices for our children. We invite you to join us in amplifying the messages of (a) starting the college admissions process early, (b) understanding the vitality and legacy of HBCUs, and (c) redefining success.

The Black Family's Guide to College Admissions

Introduction

If you are reading this book looking for the magic formula to get your child into their dream school, this is not the book for you. There is a saying in the profession of college admissions: "it's an art, not a science," meaning that it's a much more nuanced decision than one driven by numbers. Many would like to think there is a secret algorithm that can predict or guarantee admission to an elite school. There isn't. You'll find no shortcuts or "side door" in the college admissions process, even if you think you have the formula figured out. For almost every admissions decision, there are multiple factors that determine the fate of an applicant, most of which do not depend solely on numbers and have shaped an application long before it's ever submitted. While there is no formula per se, there is a playbook or road map that many college counselors and families can use to succeed in the college admissions process, and we would like to share some of it with you.

Every parent, no matter what race, wants what's "best" for their child. The bedrock on which the best is built is a child's education. From the start of our child's schooling, many of us are exhaustive in our efforts to identify the right neighborhoods to live in because they have the best public schools. If the public schools available to us do not seem satisfactory, then we may look instead into what independent or private schools we might be able to afford. This is the duty of educating a child: finding the right place for them to spend their weekdays, places where teachers and staff will care about them and help them tap into their potential as they grow into adolescents. All parents face this challenge, of course, but it can be especially challenging for Black families as they weigh the options for their child's schooling.

As a starting place, let's define success for the college search. We define it as a family and, more specifically, a student having viable college choices that will provide a fulfilling educational experience and prepare them for adult life, which is about more than just finding a job. Success is not tied to being admitted to an elite institution. Success is not associated with having a full scholarship. Success, as we see it, is when a family understands that the life of their student is precious and that they, as a family, have many options to consider. Success is finding schools where a student can be physically healthy and emotionally whole as they go through this time in their life. When colleges, plural, are in front of a teenager and their family, and they can choose where they want to go and why, they are successful.

For the better part of the past twenty-five years, we have been deeply committed to college counseling on both the secondary-school side and the college-admissions side, helping families and students navigate the college search, application, and admissions journey. Through our combined time spent working in college admissions and enrollment management, it's safe to say that there are few scenarios we have not encountered in assisting thousands of families with different goals and aspirations and in reviewing tens of thousands of applications between the two of us. In our personal and professional experiences, we understand college from the perspectives of both Historically Black Colleges and Universities (HBCUs) and predominantly white institutions (PWIs), from the viewpoints of first-generation and fourth-generation college graduates, and from attending public and private/independent secondary schools. In short, we understand that no one path or lived experience will result in success in the college admissions process. We put this book together to cover the scope of questions that Black families have, with a clear understanding that Black people are not a monolithic group but rather have a variety of experiences and perspectives.

We are Black parents first, who also happen to be college admissions professionals. We understand many of the unique questions, concerns, and needs of other Black parents approaching the college admissions process. Blacks in the United States have always had challenges in accessing higher education. As Black families, we must think about the spaces we are putting our children in and how they will be supported. We must begin to think as early as elementary school about where they should attend college, to consider public or private schooling if that is an option, and what is the best path for them given their personal, educational, and cultural needs. While these choices are not unique to Black families, they often are difficult to make when they put Black children in predominantly white environments for most of their formative years.

Given the racial history of this country and the current climate of social unrest, with campaigns in some states to erase Black history and culture from public education, Black families, who have always had to ask compelling questions about cultural safety and significance, are increasingly asking, "Should my child go to an HBCU or a PWI?" In our experience, Black families usually land in one of three camps in their answer: (1) those who believe PWIs are inherently better than HBCUs because they will offer their child a better chance at career success and more closely resemble the "real world"; (2) those with parents who attended an HBCU and want their child to follow in their footsteps and so dismiss the idea of their child attending a PWI; and (3) families who will consider *all* institutions and let the decision be guided by financial aid, location, majors offered, and ultimately what's best for their family situation. While the third camp is probably the largest, the first two make the most noise.

The debate between HBCU and PWI graduates rages on for Black parents of our generation, those who went to college in the 1980s or 1990s. Rarely would an HBCU graduate prefer a PWI for their child, yet some PWI graduates see HBCUs—especially the Black Ivies—as safe havens for their culturally confused and often "white adjacent" children. These are Black children who have gone to elementary, middle, and high school with mostly white students and feel more comfortable with them than with other Black students. The thought of going to an HBCU scares some Black children who do not think of themselves as "down" or as "having a Black card." Some would argue that it's precisely these children who should attend an HBCU to be a part of the rainbow of Black people.

Rarely have I (Shereem), a graduate of a PWI, heard an HBCU alum say they wished they had attended a PWI instead, but I have heard a lot of PWI alums say they sometimes wished they'd given more thought to attending an HBCU. One reason is that HBCU grads poke their chests out proudly, and many declare that it was the best decision of their lives. They plant seeds of HBCU love in their children at an early age, and some parents unwaveringly predetermine that their child will attend their alma mater or that their money will go only to an HBCU. Tim, for instance, has claimed that his son will go to Morehouse College, even though he has spent three times as many years at Emory University as he did at Morehouse and his children would go to Emory for free if admitted!

We cannot tell you how many times in our work as admissions professionals we have been asked where we went to school. A Black college graduate's answer to that question will attract judgment, regardless of what it is. If you went to an HBCU, there will be those who think your education was inferior to those who attended a PWI. And if you attended a PWI, there will be those who'll question why you made that choice and doubt your knowledge of racial inequalities in America.

If we think about success in financial terms, HBCUs deserve more credit than they receive in mainstream white media.

Tennessee State University (HBCU)
Nashville, TN
6,000 Undergraduates
Public
Graduate Students: Yes
Setting: Urban

University of Central Missouri (PWI)
Warrensburg, MO
10,000 Undergraduates
Public
Graduate Students: Yes
Setting: Remote

Columbia University (PWI)
New York, NY
6,200 Undergraduates
Private
Graduate Students: Yes
Setting: Urban

Princeton University (PWI)
Princeton, NJ
5,300 Undergraduates
Private
Graduate Students: Yes
Setting: Suburban

Few billionaires have influenced the world as much as Oprah Winfrey, one of the richest Black people on the globe, who attended Tennessee State University, an HBCU; or Black billionaire businessman David Steward, who attended the University of Central Missouri, a PWI. However, if you measure success by accomplishments, you could

point to President Barack Obama and First Lady Michelle Obama, who attended Columbia University and Princeton University, respectively. The list of successful Black college graduates, from both HBCUs and PWIs, is extensive, and we will highlight many of them throughout the book.

The debate over which type of school is "best" for our children is ongoing. However, what has become clear to us is that Black students should find the best school of whichever type to nurture their development and identity and feed their academic souls. If choosing a college to attend was as simple as thinking about majors, financial aid, the college's location, and its rate of job placement, we would not be writing this book. We know that there is much more to the decision, and that's why the question about which college type to choose is so complicated to answer. Given the number of times we have heard the question, we have learned to highlight the strengths of both institutional types. But we are also aware of what the family really wants to know—which is better?—and we always end our answer with "it all depends on what the student is looking for." Some families are simply looking for the best school to prepare their student for a postgraduate career, while other families are thinking about the student's identity and how the college environment will help shape their entire life.

Preparatory Research

For the past three years, as we prepared to write this book, we conducted interviews, facilitated roundtable discussions, administered surveys, and traveled the country engaging with Black parents who expect their children to go to college. Many of the parents went to HBCUs, and others went to PWIs. While we heard a range of opinions on the value of education and how to construct an educational trajectory, there were common themes: safety—mental, emotional, and physical—and preparation for the process. Black families told us they do not feel as informed about the college admissions process as they want to be, and they often blamed the school their child attends. Most were clear that they would not predetermine where their child would go, but many were also aware that the chasm between an HBCU and a PWI experience is wide and they, ultimately, want what's best for their child. One thing that we did find alarming, however, was that of the Black parents we surveyed, 94 percent believe there is a perception that PWIs are superior to HBCUs.

We also spent a significant amount of time talking with college counselors from both public and independent high schools to hear how Black families are treated in the college preparation process. We asked the counselors, mostly white, what HBCUs they were familiar with and if they encouraged their Black students to apply. Most were candid and sheepishly admitted that they were not familiar with HBCUs apart from the Black Ivies (Morehouse, Spelman, and Howard) and that they could do better.

Arrangement of the Book

This book was designed to provide a road map and educational resource for Black families who want to understand the experience of college search and college admissions. To explain it, we arranged the book in three parts. Part I focuses on the *context* of higher education for Black students looking to go to college. There are several variables that will influence the colleges and universities that families consider long before students enter high school. We discuss how parents can think about primary and secondary education, whether an HBCU or a PWI may be the better choice for your child, and what particular institutions will provide the best return on investment and career opportunities for your child, if that is a priority. Before you begin to think about what institutions you will be looking at, we believe it is essential to ask what college can offer your child beyond an education alone. We also think it's critical to discuss the current higher education landscape and any external factors that may influence what schools you'll consider and how those schools will evaluate your child. One such factor is the Supreme Court's decision in 2023 against affirmative action in college admissions.

Part II focuses on the *X factors* to be considered in college admissions. We begin with what questions you and your family should be asking, examine some of the areas that can cause anxiety and tension in the college search process, and consider gender inequities, identity, and other concerns that may require a specific path or considerations. We also examine what families should be thinking about if their student is an athlete or artist or has another talent that will guide their college search. Finally, we bring up one of the biggest considerations in the college admissions process: money. How families address these X factors will be critical to identifying schools that will be a good fit for their student.

In part III we focus on the college admissions *process* itself, which should begin a lot earlier than most of us want to believe. We address how to make the most out of college visits, how to manage the relationship between a school's college counseling office and your family, and how standardized testing factors in the process. We also get into the nuts and bolts of the college application and do a deep dive into the importance of writing application essays with an authentic voice. We not only provide you with a guide through the process, from start to finish, more importantly we provide the insight and resources you and your family will need to feel confident about applying to college. Following part III, you'll find appendixes and other additional resources.

Things to Keep in Mind as You Read This Book

We have summarized below some of the most important messages of the book.

Guide your child. Their own self-awareness is key, but you, as their parent, also have to steer them in the college admissions process.

Explore different interests, strengths, majors, careers, and colleges. Nothing is more important than being open-minded in the college admissions process. With some four thousand colleges and universities in the United States, there are plenty to choose from.

Encourage self-advocacy. Your child has to step up in the college search. While we want you to be a copilot, your child has to want this more than you want it for them.

Examine the differences between HBCUs and PWIs. Culturally, educationally, and financially, there are elements that need to be fully evaluated.

Execute excellent applications and essays. This is not to be taken lightly. Whether it's for a college or a scholarship, have your child put significant time and effort into preparing the best possible profile that will make them stand out.

Ensure you have choices. College admissions success means having college choices. Then you and your child get to consider what their life plan should be for the next five to ten years.

Free Online Resources

Explore these resources when you begin the college admissions process.

College Search
Bigfuture.collegeboard.org

Cappex.com

Collegereview.com

CollegeXPress.com

Niche.com

Princetonreview.com

Uncf.org

Unigo.com

Financial Aid
Bold.org

Fastweb.com

FinAid.org

Finaideapp.com

Goingmerry.com

Meritmore.com

Myscholly.com

Nextstudentloans.com

Raise.me

Salliemae.com

Scholarshipamerica.org

Scholarshiphelp.org

Scholarships.com

Studentaid.gov

Wiredscholar.com

Testing
ACT.org

Akilbello.com

Collegeboard.com

Fairtest.org

Mathsp.com

General
Coalitionforcollegeaccess.org

Collegeboard.com

Commonapp.org

Commonblackcollegeapp.com

Ctcl.com

Jennthetutor.com

Nacacnet.org

Ncaa.org

Possefoundation.org

Questbridge.org

Strategicadmissionsadvice.com

PART I

Context

CHAPTER 1

Affirmative Action Is Dead

Overview

In June 2023 the US Supreme Court struck down a decades-old precedent when it ruled that most colleges and universities could no longer legally consider race as a factor in their admissions decisions. Black families should weigh the consequences of this ruling when they are making plans for their child's college education.

Deeming race irrelevant in law does not make it so in life . . .
and having so detached itself from this country's actual past
and present experiences, the Court has now been lured
into interfering with the crucial work that UNC and other
institutions of higher learning are doing to solve America's
real-world problems.

—Justice Ketanji Brown Jackson

Heavy on our minds as we revised this book for its second edition was the ruling by the US Supreme Court that said colleges and universities can no longer take race into consideration as a specific basis for granting admission. Published on June 29, 2023, this historic decision overturned a long-standing precedent that benefited millions of students, not just Black and Brown students. The court handed down its decision after hearing a pair of related cases: one lawsuit against Harvard University, a private school, and another against the University of North Carolina, Chapel Hill, a state-funded public school. In our opinion, this decision dealt a devastating blow to tremendous progress that had been made over the past five decades. With emotions still raw and all of the decision's effects not yet known, we cannot say exactly what it will mean for our children.

Yes, we are disappointed, but we are not surprised. We believe this decision will impact Black students' educational opportunities and possibly impede their professional growth. We've been here before, though, so we will remain resilient. We must continue to fight the racism in educational segregation that aims to deprive young people of access to information that can change their lives.

To be clear, other preferences in admissions—legacy, philanthropic, and athletic—remain intact to date. This speaks volumes about how some influential members of our government view Black students. We are allowed to run, block, dribble, and hit a ball or go to war (military academies can still consider race in admissions), but when we apply our minds rather than our bodies, we are a threat whose race must now be ignored by law. This makes us question why we place so much emphasis on the colleges and universities that were never built to educate Black students in the first place.

We, along with others who value diversity, equity, inclusion, and belonging in college admissions and in the college experience, will continue to uphold and believe in the importance of higher education for all. For our children, however, we must reexamine our intentions and options and, ultimately, redefine success.

Affirmative Action of the Past

Since the founding of the United States, race has always been a factor. The ending of slavery and the dismantling of the "separate but equal" doctrine that prevailed for most of the twentieth century, and that necessitated the creation of Historically Black Colleges and Universities, did not remove racism from the fabric of American society. The Civil Rights Act of 1964 prohibited racial discrimination in public places, provided for the integration of schools and other public facilities, and made employment discrimination illegal.

The following year, in 1965, the Higher Education Act was passed to strengthen the educational resources of colleges and universities and to provide financial assistance to students in postsecondary education. This act enabled many to attend college who would otherwise not have had the chance. These two bills were the most sweeping civil rights legislation passed since Reconstruction, and many thought they would end the need to center conversations around race in higher education. That thought, however, turned out to be a wish at odds with reality.

Soon after the civil rights movement of the 1960s, affirmative action emerged as a response to historical discrimination and systemic inequalities that had evolved over time. Affirmative action was the name given to policies and practices in higher education aimed at promoting diversity and providing equal opportunities for historically marginalized groups. Those groups included racial and ethnic minorities, women, and individuals from financially disadvantaged backgrounds. These policies called for considering factors such as race, ethnicity, gender, or socioeconomic status as one of many criteria in college admissions.

The first lawsuit contesting affirmative action went before the Supreme Court in 1978. The case of *Regents of the University of California v. Bakke* set a legal precedent for affirmative action in higher education. The court recognized the importance of diversity on campuses and allowed for the consideration of race as one factor among many in admissions decisions. It did, however, place limitations on the extent to which race could be used as a factor. From 1978 to 2023, affirmative action in higher education faced more legal challenges and continued to be a subject of debate. Supporters argued that the consideration of race helps to redress historical disadvantages and fosters diverse learning environments, while opponents raised concerns about fairness, merit-based admissions, and potential "reverse racism." Over this period of time, the Supreme Court allowed, with narrowing scope, the continued consideration of race as a factor in college admissions. This all changed, though, with the court's June 2023 decision, which will determine the treatment of race in higher education admissions for the foreseeable future.

Many Black people born between 1960 and 2005 who attended predominantly white institutions were beneficiaries of affirmative action, me (Shereem) included. I have often asked myself if I should have been admitted to Wesleyan University in the fall of 1991 as an Early Decision candidate. I was, after all, a B/B− student who did not break 1000 on the SAT. At the time and to this day, Wesleyan is one of the most selective liberal arts schools in the country, by its published admissions standards, and I was not academically qualified. But I applied anyway because I believed in my extracurricular activities and leadership and had two high school friends a year ahead of me who were already there. Wesleyan was where I wanted to be, and because of the school's institutional priorities and commitment to diversity, I was admitted.

Now, did I deserve to be admitted based on academic accomplishments? Maybe, maybe not. But the word *deserve* is tricky here given legacy and development (philanthropic) cases where applicants have benefited from nepotism in college admissions for centuries. There is documented history of white students who did not deserve to be admitted to the same colleges their parents or grandparents went to but who got in anyway. This includes former presidents of the United States. Even worse, there are students who get admitted to elite schools because someone in their family knows "someone on the board" who advocated for their admission. But that's a longer, uglier discussion for another day. Back to my story.

While attending Wesleyan, I studied abroad in Kenya, played on the basketball team for a year, pledged a fraternity, learned how to write better, and graduated in four years. I believe I took advantage of an educational opportunity, made the campus a better place, and, as an alumnus, have made the university proud. Wesleyan's administrators took a chance on me, and I proved them right. This was the theory behind the landmark book *The Shape of the River: Long-Term*

Consequences of Considering Race in College and University Admissions, by William G. Bowen and Derek Bok,* published in 1998. This book analyzes the impact of affirmative action policies in higher education and argues in favor of race-conscious admissions.

When I was an undergraduate, my advisor happened to be Wesleyan's dean of admission, and I worked for the admissions office one summer as a tour guide. When I was later made aware of Bowen and Bok's book, I was probably two years out of college and already finding myself intrigued by college counseling. The book affirmed for me that I had been qualified for admission to Wesleyan. These two titans of higher education put forth ample evidence showing that race-conscious admissions leads to more diverse and inclusive educational and, ultimately, professional environments that enhance learning experiences, promote cross-cultural understanding, and prepare people for living in a diverse society. Additionally, expanding access to higher education for historically underrepresented minority groups can help to remedy past inequalities and create opportunities for students who may have faced barriers to education. But the part that blew me away was the authors telling me my life story of educational outcomes: that a student admitted through a race-conscious policy, when provided with necessary support and resources, can perform as well as or better than their peers.

So, in our opinion, race-conscious admissions takes as a critical step toward "leveling the playing field." The time elapsed from 1960 to 2020 is only sixty years, and that does not make up for four hundred years of racial cruelty, injustice, and discrimination, but it's a start. We still want to see compensatory justice (reparation) to

---

* Derek Bok is an American lawyer, educator, and author who served as the president of Harvard University for two separate terms, from 1971 to 1991, and again as interim president in 2006. William G. Bowen was an American economist, educator, and former president of Princeton University from 1972 to 1988. He later served as the president of the Andrew W. Mellon Foundation. The work of these two former Ivy League presidents has had a notable impact on the understanding of higher education access, diversity, and the long-term effects of affirmative action policies.

rectify past and ongoing injustices by providing equal opportunities to those who have been historically marginalized.

Selective schools over the past thirty years have proclaimed their commitment to "holistic admissions," where multiple factors are considered: race or ethnicity along with other qualities, achievements, and experiences. These schools contend that focusing solely on standardized test scores and grades may overlook valuable qualities and potential in applicants from underrepresented backgrounds. Without race-conscious admissions, the goal of leveling the playing field may be in jeopardy, and the constituency on college campuses may no longer reflect the diverse society these institutions serve, which we think would be unfortunate.

The bottom line is that affirmative action raised the enrollment and representation of Black students at predominantly white institutions. It contributed to more racially diverse student bodies, to enhanced educational experiences, and to more inclusive learning environments. Please note that we acknowledge the intersection of race with socioeconomic status. While affirmative action may have benefited Black students, individuals from lower socioeconomic backgrounds within the Black community may face additional challenges in accessing and succeeding in higher education. Addressing broader economic disparities in American society requires comprehensive approaches beyond affirmative action alone.

Affirmative Action after the 2023 Ruling

On June 29, 2023, the Supreme Court voted six to three in declaring practices of race-conscious admissions unconstitutional, while ignoring decades of legal precedent, facts, and testimony. What this means for higher education moving forward is uncertain, and all the ramifications won't be known for years. What this means for you moving forward, however, is clear. Students and families will have to be intentional about the schools they choose to apply to, at the time they begin planning for college admissions and later when students go about presenting themselves in their applications, especially in their essays.

One of the biggest ironies of the court's decision is that it focused on two of the most selective schools in the country: Harvard, which has an admit rate under 5 percent (meaning that 95 percent of its applicants are not admitted), and the University of North Carolina at Chapel Hill, with an admit rate of about 20 percent, which is driven downward by a state mandate limiting out-of-state students. Both institutions are in the top 1 percent of selectivity in the country; this means that the basis for the court's decision did not reflect the larger landscape of higher education. Going forward, students and families should not rely on the institutional rankings of *U.S. News and World Report* in deciding what schools make the cut. We also think that Black students and families should give even more consideration to Historically Black Colleges and Universities than they might have before. These institutions may become the de facto option for many Black students, as they were for most of the nineteenth and twentieth centuries. Appendix A of this book lists Best Colleges for Black Students, which can help you think through what schools to consider.

Following the court's decision, we have intensified our customary urging to families to start discussing the college admissions process *early*. The court's decision will affect how colleges review applications and so, in turn, how families build a college list. Yet to be determined is how the decision will affect institutions' allocation of financial aid. Given these unknowns, families should begin researching schools and scholarships and preparing for standardized tests and application essays no later than junior year if possible. If you are already a high school senior or are the parent of one, you still have time, but not much; we refer you to chapter 14, "Expectation-for-Success Timeline," to help you make the most of the time you have for preparation.

What may be the biggest outcome of this decision is an increased emphasis on the application essay in college admissions.

While essays have always been an important part of an application, given the changes in how schools will have to review applications, what essays reveal about applicants may be even more critical. Accordingly, we have written a new chapter for the second edition titled "The Power of Essay Writing" with advice on how an applicant can stand out when telling their story. Too often in essays students simply share their extracurricular activities in narrative form, and that may not be enough. What's worse, their narrative may do no more than repeat what appears elsewhere in the application. We encourage students to write about their distinct lived experience, which may relate to their cultural identity. Through this amplification of authenticity, students share how they are unique and what they can add to a college community in addition to their intellectual horsepower.

> *Nothing in this opinion should be construed as prohibiting*
> *universities from considering an applicant's discussion of*
> *how race affected his or her life, be it through discrimination,*
> *inspiration, or otherwise.*
>
> —Chief Justice John Roberts

Is this decision the end of the world? No. Black students will still be able to access higher education and go on to great success, but we are at a reflection point. There are questions Black families need to ask: Why do we hold selective colleges and universities, most of which are predominantly white, in such high esteem? Will attending one of these schools truly benefit our child's academic, social, and emotional development? Would attending an HBCU provide our child with an education even more meaningful and useful? Former First Lady Michelle Obama tweeted her thoughts on affirmative action right after the court released its decision:

> *"Back in college, I was one of the few Black students on my campus,*
> *and I was proud of getting into such a respected school. I knew*

I'd worked hard for it. But still, I sometimes wondered if people thought I got there because of affirmative action. It was a shadow that students like me couldn't shake, whether those doubts came from the outside or inside our own minds.

But the fact is this: I belonged. And semester after semester, decade after decade, for more than half a century, countless students like me showed they belonged, too. It wasn't just the kids of color who benefitted, either. Every student who heard a perspective they might not have encountered, who had an assumption challenged, who had their minds and their hearts opened gained a lot as well. It wasn't perfect, but there's no doubt that it helped offer new ladders of opportunity for those who, throughout our history, have too often been denied a chance to show how fast they can climb."

Michelle Obama also pointed out that even as the Supreme Court outlawed race-based college admissions, the law still allows colleges to consider other factors such as legacy status, donor and employee relationships, and recruitment for athletics. "We don't usually question if those students belong," she wrote. "So often, we just accept that money, power, and privilege are perfectly justifiable forms of affirmative action, while kids growing up like I did are expected to compete when the ground is anything but level."

Her words are bold and we like them. They contribute to what will be an ongoing conversation after the court's decision and one we are honored to continue.

CHAPTER 2

Black Parents

The Choices We Make Now Matter Later

Overview

Black parents who are college graduates, especially first-generation college graduates, want our children to have more than we did, and their education is central to that. Many of us believe it is our duty to consider how we achieved our educational success and then take it a step farther with our children. This often means sending our children to private schools or moving to a more affluent suburb in search of better educational options. The goal of these choices is often to expose our children to a more rigorous academic curriculum on their educational trajectory to a good college and beyond.

Along the way, though, we may compromise culture and community. Is this *right*? Is this *good*? How does this affect our children, not just emotionally, but in their chances for college admissions success? And are there other potential consequences to these decisions? This chapter explores how parents' choices at early stages of their child's education affect their college counseling and ultimately their college choices.

Parents ask questions about where and how to educate their children before their children are born. Parents elated to be pregnant start planning everything from their child's baby shower to their wedding. Every parent declares they want what's best for their child and will offer them all the things they themselves did not have and more. Parents often try to replicate all the advantages of their own upbringing, if they had them, that helped them find success. We all do it; it's just the nature of being a parent. We want to protect our children from any harm and give them the world while doing it. There is no one definitive guide to parenting, and each child is different and will experience the world in different ways. We parents are a collection of our personal experiences, and we use those experiences, both good and bad, to help chart a path for our children to succeed in life. A day does not go by when we as parents don't have to make a decision about our children, but the decision-making about our children's education and college preparation should start earlier rather than later. These decisions often aren't made overnight and require hard conversations, resources, and in most instances with Black families, some sense of compromise.

Black parents want for their children what everyone else wants: to be better and to have more. But what does that mean and to what expense or extent? We want our children to lead lives with few regrets, have enriching and rewarding friendships, and, yes, obtain financial assets. We understand that much of the training for success happens in the home and in school as early as elementary. We are committed to putting our children around other children and families that are upwardly mobile and financially rewarded. Many of our choices, especially early on, are about who will care for and teach our children. If we are financially able to, many of us have chosen to live in places where the educational options are good. Public schools serve communities, and the taxpaying populations surrounding these schools expect the schools to elevate their children. Often we Black parents choose an area to live in after we have thoroughly vetted its public schools. Many parents are willing to pay higher property taxes or even rent a house in a school district that they believe will benefit their child. Unfortunately, what frequently happens is that these neighborhoods are not as diverse with other Black people as we would like them to be. The educational resources of affluent white neighborhoods dwarf those of predominantly Black neighborhoods in most cases, and for us to have access to these rich resources, we parents may have to decide to be "the onlys" or one of a few Black families in a whiter, richer community. This is not an easy choice because we are placing our children in predominantly white neighborhoods and schools just to be . . . "better?"

> "We knew when we moved to our suburban neighborhood 18 years ago that we were moving into a predominantly white area, but we were moving there for the property value and school system. While our son's education has not been without issue, as a Black parent those are just some of the decisions you have to make; you will take 80 percent good and know there is going to be 20 percent bad."

Given how much college preparation has changed over the last twenty years, we feel it's important to provide Black parents insight into how their educational and school choices can affect the college admissions process.

Where Should I Send My Child to School?

I (Tim) can recall an occasion when I was out with a friend in Atlanta who is an executive at an investment bank. As we were talking, he casually asked me, "What is the best high school for my children to go to?" At that time, I believe, his oldest was twelve. Given his success in his profession, I knew he had asked the question with no concern about money; rather, he wanted to know how best to position his children for success beyond college. Knowing that he lived in Buckhead, an affluent part of Atlanta, I told him to save his money and send his children to North Atlanta High School, a public school, have them enroll in the International Baccalaureate program, and they will be in good stead. He then mentioned some private schools and asked, "Why not them instead?" My response was simple: "Do you want them to get a good education, or do you want to tell your friends they go to private school?" He paused before he responded and then said that he wanted them to go where they will be prepared to succeed at any college. I said North Atlanta was the right place then; it has long been known for its International Baccalaureate and Advanced Placement programs and the good academic preparation of its students. As Emory University's longtime admissions representative for Atlanta, I knew firsthand that no college that recruits in Atlanta does not make it a priority to stop there for the quality and diversity of the student population. My friend's oldest child did go to North Atlanta High School, and the family was highly satisfied with the educational experience she had there.

When a senior in 2022, she was admitted to almost all the colleges she applied to, including selective schools like Georgetown and Emory. She ultimately decided to stay in Atlanta and attend Spelman College, where she received a scholarship. Her mother had attended Spelman and her father Morehouse. When asked why she chose Spelman, she responded, "I wanted to be somewhere where I was not just challenged academically but also could develop as a person in a nurturing environment. Spelman College is that perfect fit for me."

I went through the same thought process that my friend did when I considered my own children's education. They spent their toddler years in a Montessori school, and we were very pleased with the education they received. However, with my wife and I having attended public school, we were adamant about them transitioning eventually to a public school. As they approached the age when children begin kindergarten, we thought that would be a great time to execute our plan, but we did not know how complicated it would be. From beginning to end the process took place over six stressful months. In identifying public schools that we felt good about our children going to, we found that they were either in neighborhoods we could not afford, were out in the suburbs where we did not want to live, or did not have the diversity we were looking for. As we continued our search, we knew we were going to have to make some compromises. As for the option of keeping them in their current school, we were finding that the rising cost of the school would not be sustainable for us, and we just had to make a decision. Ultimately, we found a school in a neighborhood we liked that met every criterion we had, but we ended up renting an older, smaller home in the neighborhood to make it work. While it was a small compromise to make in the larger scheme of things, we are somewhat at the mercy of the home's owners. These were the decisions we had to make about our children's elementary school.

My friend and I were fortunate enough to have several choices by living in Atlanta, and he and his family had considerable resources at their disposal. We recognize the privilege that comes with being able to have these educational options. Not all families have as many options. Most parents are presented with choices of public schools that don't have resources comparable to those of private schools. In some cases there are charter school options, but many have no guarantee of admission and often bring additional challenges such as transportation and limited extracurricular options. Parents also have to consider the environment in which their children will be educated. Private schools may have many resources to support students, yet they often lack the diversity that many Black families are looking for. These are the challenges that can shape academic preparation and identity formation.

Just so that we are clear, we are not implying that private schools are better than public or charter schools; we are just acknowledging that in many instances there are trade-offs in the choices we make as parents. Some trade-offs are hard to accept. To put your students in the best possible educational position, you must address these questions in elementary and middle school. The academic preparation students receive in those formative years sets the foundation for their high school courses. In part III, "Process," we provide a lot more context for how the foundation formed in elementary and middle school can impact students' performance in high school courses, their college preparation, and how competitive they will be in college admissions.

"My children began in a suburban public school, but after a couple of racial incidents with my son we decided to move them to private school. While he was an all-A student in public school, when he moved to private school, his grades dropped. He ended up doing well and enrolling in a good college, but he did not have as many options as we would have liked. At the same time we had some family friends that had kids the same age as ours that left their kids in the public school system that we moved from, and they had several more options than my son did. While I know there are other things at play, I could not help but ask myself, 'Did I do the right thing moving him into a private school?'"

In the table at the end of the chapter we share the model a parent developed to help his family evaluate the pros and cons of moving their child from public to private school. The model gives evidence of how early and to what extent some parents think about their children's education and the factors they consider.

Preparing to Think about College

The question of school choice is one that we all ask at some point as parents because it is more than a choice about education alone; it is also about the development, safety, and well-being of our children. It is critical that Black parents understand that almost everything their child does from middle school through high school influences their college options. Whether it is course selection, standardized testing, assorted activities, or the experiences that students write about in their application essays, Black parents need to be aware that everything matters. The college search and application process does not start in the eleventh grade. It starts with exposure to what college is; the activities and classes that students have in elementary school and middle school may affect their activities and courses in high school. It pains us that too many Black parents depend on what they know from twenty or thirty years ago when they applied and went to college. Much of that is not relevant for what your child will go through. Your children will never wait in line to register for classes, fill out a paper application, and, depending on your situation, may never have to know where the office of financial aid is or have to wait on a refund check.

Yale University (PWI)
New Haven, CT
6,792 Undergraduates
Private
Graduate Students: Yes
Setting: Midsize City

Brown University (PWI)
Providence, RI
6,200 Undergraduates
Private
Graduate Students: Yes
Setting: Urban

Dartmouth College (PWI)
Hanover, NH
4,600 Undergraduates
Private
Graduate Students: Yes
Setting: Remote

Harvard University (PWI)
Cambridge, MA
5,200 Undergraduates
Private
Graduate Students: Yes
Setting: Urban

We want Black parents to be *drivers* of their children's college search and application process. In his best-selling book *Who Gets In and Why: A Year inside College Admissions*, author Jeffrey Selingo defines *drivers* as voracious consumers of information, those who read guidebooks or regularly talk to college counselors or others who can help them, as opposed to *passengers*, who are simply along for the ride through the admissions process. Being a driver means "taking the wheel" and steering your children toward the kinds of schools you think may be best for them given who they are. We want to give you the information to make informed decisions as early as you need to make them so that your child has the educational and life options they want for themselves. This is how other cultural groups are winning in the college application process. They understand that the traditional selection process continues to favor families that focus on advanced high school courses, test scores, and distinctive extracurricular activities. Pop culture would have you believe that "diversity" trumps all in PWI college admissions, whether racial diversity or diversity from first-generation college students. This is simply not true. Many colleges enroll students from a multitude of socioeconomic backgrounds, which is key to achieving diversity in higher education.

However, in a 2021 article in the *Atlantic*, author Caitlin Flanagan revealed that although less than 2 percent of the nation's students attend so-called independent schools (a type of private school), 24 percent of Yale's class of 2024 attended an independent school. At Princeton, that figure is 25 percent. At Brown and Dartmouth, it is even higher, at 29 percent. The numbers are even more astonishing when you consider that the students are not distributed evenly across the country's more than 1,600 independent schools; instead, they are concentrated in the most exclusive ones. The Dalton School in New York City has sent about a third of its graduates to the Ivy League in the past five years. Ditto for the Spence School in New York City. Harvard-Westlake, in Los Angeles, sent forty-five kids to Harvard alone. Noble and Greenough School, in Massachusetts, did even better: fifty kids went to Harvard. These numbers show that where you send your child to high school can impact where they later go to college.

When we spoke to families before writing this book, many assumed that being Black and having good grades and test scores equals automatic admission to the most selective PWIs. This is not so. What most institutions want is diversity, and that can come in different forms. Offering educational opportunity to historically underrepresented populations is critical to achieving diversity, which may mean that, if your child enjoyed educational and extracurricular opportunities that other applicants did not, your child may be viewed as just another applicant, regardless of their race or ethnicity.

Many assume that PWIs need Black students. No. What most colleges and universities are looking for is diversity, and that comes in many forms. One of the biggest forms of diversity that institutions are looking for is socioeconomic diversity. So while there is a kind of diversity that a Black student can bring to campus, if their mother is a doctor and father is a lawyer and that student attended private school, an admissions officer may wonder whether this student will really bring a different perspective to campus more so than someone from another background who did not have as many op-portunities. Thus, depending on your situation, you may think your child will bring diversity to a school, but in fact your child could be looked on as just another privileged applicant.

Another point we need to emphasize is this: if having elite col-lege options is important to you as a parent and you are choosing to impart your values and opinions to your child, *you must start this process early*. It can be lengthy, and having a clear story and high grades and test scores, which may require tutoring, as well as an array of extracurricular activities helps tremendously. If you are the parent of a young child and as yet have no clear idea who your child will be academically, culturally, or what they will like to do, this will be hard to predict. But for those who have a child in late middle school or the early years of high school, knowing who they are and exploring the range of educational opportunities you have will help your child as they take the next steps.

The path to college is a long one, and depending on the col-lege options your family is looking at, you may have to make some important decisions long before you thought you had to. Even if you don't dream of your child going to a top-tier school, the earlier that you as a family begin to think about the process of applying and going to college, the more options you will have available to you. We have found in our experience that there are fewer and fewer "guarantees" nowadays when it comes to college admissions. Some schools that twenty years ago admitted students at a high rate have since become more selective, so you can no longer assume that a school will consider you a legacy or that a school needs Black stu-dents. In many instances that is not the case. The process of college preparation needs to start now.

Example of a Pro and Con Analysis of Public versus Independent (Private) School

Panel A. Priorities for Sally's Education

Priority	Description
Education fundamentals	Ensure Sally establishes a firm foundation in reading, math, and writing
In-person instruction	Keep Sally in in-person schooling
COVID safety	COVID protocols must be sufficient to keep us safe within reason
Size & resources	School should not be overlarge and should have resources for plentiful extracurricular activities
Reasonable cost	Must be affordable for us
Diversity	School should expose Sally to diverse backgrounds across the student body, faculty leadership, and curriculum
High school's reputation	School's reputation should position Sally to be competitive in her college applications
Convenience	Ensure Mom has a reasonable and sustainable daily routine to get the children to/from school

Example of a Pro and Con Analysis of Public versus Independent (Private) School (*continued*)

Panel B. Scenario 1: Live in Current Home and Compare Local Public School with Independent School

Priority	Weight	Local public school	Score: 1 (con) → 6 (pro)	Independent school	Score: 1 (con) → 6 (pro)
Education fundamentals	0.2	▸ Overall the curriculum is probably on par with the independent school in the primary grades. ▸ Students in Sally's class are behind because of COVID. Teachers will struggle to help performing students advance because they are likely to be preoccupied with struggling students. This dynamic is unlikely to resolve itself in the near term. Additional tutoring will be required for Sally.	3	▸ Presents the opportunity for high-caliber schooling if you are in the advanced track, but the school does track. If you are just taking regular classes, there is limited educational benefit. ▸ Outside tutoring and support will likely be needed to ensure Sally lands in the advanced track. ▸ One of the teachers at the independent school seemed very drab, but there is apparently no way to request the teacher you want.	4
COVID safety / In-person instruction	0.2	▸ School has stronger COVID protocols than the independent school (weekly testing and daily temp checks). ▸ School's track record from last year suggests some risk that the school could close again if the virus gets bad. That said, this year we have vaccines, and the teachers are vaccinated, so a full closure is probably unlikely.	3	▸ School doesn't do daily temp checks or weekly testing. Is very disciplined about masks and social distancing in the class-rooms. ▸ School unlikely to close.	4

Priority	Weight	Local public school	Score: 1 (con) → 6 (pro)	Independent school	Score: 1 (con) → 6 (pro)
Size & resources	0.15	▸ School is large overall and perhaps bigger than ideal for Sally. ▸ Has resources but in limited supply. Getting access requires parents to be very proactive and engaged.	4	▸ School is smaller overall and more of an ideal size for Sally and the level of attention/support she often thrives in. ▸ Many more accessible and enriching extra-curricular activities that Sally will enjoy.	6
Reasonable cost	0.15	▸ Free tuition. ▸ Will need to spend dollars on wraparound services; could easily spend $12K/year on these support services; that said, they will be 1-on-1 and won't be subsidizing programs for other folks.	5	▸ $25K/year; coupled with second child's schooling, we'll be spending $50K/year on primary education. From now to graduation, we'd be committing ~$250K–$275K. ▸ If additional 1-on-1 support (tutoring, etc.) is needed to increase probability that Sally lands in the advanced track, that's on top of tuition expense.	1
Diversity	0.1	▸ Very diverse across faculty and leadership. ▸ More middle-/ upper-middle-class Brown kids attend school. Sally is likely to have friends across the spectrum of background and experience.	5	▸ Most diverse of similar private schools (in both faculty and student body). ▸ Kids in a similar socioeconomic status at independent school more likely to be white; could jeopardize Sally's self-esteem. ▸ Alumni shared tough stories of how they were treated; the head of school responded with meaningful action.	3

(continued)

Example of a Pro and Con Analysis of Public versus Independent (Private) School (*continued*)

Priority	Weight	Local public school	Score: 1 (con) → 6 (pro)	Independent school	Score: 1 (con) → 6 (pro)
High school's reputation	0.1	▸ Local public school is viewed as a great school by college admissions officers. If Sally is on an equivalent track at local public school, her odds of entry are on par or better than at the independent school.	4	▸ Independent school does not advantage or disadvantage students on college applications. It really will come down to what track Sally ends up on and how she performs. ▸ The independent school's name drives more impact in social circles than in college admissions.	4
Convenience	0.1	▸ 2 min. from the house; she can eventually walk to school. ▸ She gets the benefit of living in the neighborhood with schoolmates.	6	▸ Basically infeasible to get both Sally and her sibling to and from school each day without additional help. ▸ Carpooling adds risk (not comfortable having Sally ride with someone we don't know). ▸ If we move to a different part of the city, the busing option increases convenience considerably.	1
Weighted Total			4.05		3.45

Panel C. Further Considerations

Input from others

S: "If local public school was an option, I probably wouldn't be at the independent school."

T: "Independent school is a large school where people go for the name. The education really isn't that different and not worth the price."

R: "My kids coming from local public school knew more than the kids from the independent school." [There's a question about what track the kids were on.]

Wildcards

▸ Future moves / neighborhood: If we move, then local public school becomes a lot less convenient, and we may end up in private school. In that scenario, we are better off switching to the independent school now, assuming we can sort out the logistics. At some point in the future, Sally would have to test into the independent school.

▸ Decision speed: Making the decision to switch this quickly feels hasty. What are the consequences of deferring for a year?

▸ Decision correction: If we leave local public school, there is no guarantee that we can get Sally back in.

CHAPTER 3

Shift in Power

The Resurgence of HBCU Culture

Overview

HBCUs have been an integral part of American higher education, given the United States' long history of racism and segregation. For decades, these institutions have been the foundations for Black achievement and excellence—from Thurgood Marshall to Toni Morrison to Langston Hughes. For the most part, conversations about HBCUs were limited in mainstream media following the Civil Rights Act of 1964. While there has always been a segment of the population that has recognized the value and importance of HBCUs, now more than ever they are being featured and celebrated in American popular culture because of the current emphasis on empowering racial differences and a variety of celebrity endorsements. This chapter examines the reasons that HBCUs have seen a resurgence in popularity.

In the words of James Todd Smith, better known as LL Cool J, "Don't call it a comeback / I've been here for years." While some people may just now be paying attention to HBCUs, they have been a staple in US higher education since 1837, when Cheyney University in Pennsylvania opened its doors as the first HBCU, although Lincoln University, also in Pennsylvania, claims to be the first degree-granting HBCU after it opened in 1854. This point of contention over primacy has been going on since the schools were founded. Regardless, HBCUs have been a critical means for Black students to obtain a college degree in the United States for almost two hundred years.

Following desegregation, Black colleges continued to serve as the foundation for access to college for Black students, but some of the honor and prestige that historically came from attending these schools began to shift given the new options that became available to Black students. For much of the latter part of the twentieth century, coverage and discussions about HBCUs were limited. However, in the 1980s and 1990s HBCUs made an appearance in popular culture in films like *School Daze* (1988), which provided the world with a glimpse of attending a Black college. At around that same time the world was introduced to what some would argue is the greatest and most influential HBCU of all: Hillman College. A fictional college and the setting for the sitcom *A Different World*, Hillman College made an impact on a generation of students.

Cheyney University (HBCU)
Cheyney, PA
600 Undergraduates
Public
Graduate Students: Yes
Setting: Suburban

Lincoln University (HBCU)
Lincoln, PA
1,900 Undergraduates
Public
Graduate Students: Yes
Setting: Remote

On Thursday nights for six years, from 1987 to 1993, America got the privilege of seeing an array of young Black people enjoying the challenges and triumphs of college life. *A Different World*, a spin-off of *The Cosby Show*, was transformational for depicting the distinctive culture of an HBCU. The show used Spelman College as a backdrop for some footage of the fictional Hillman College. Although not real in the physical sense, Hillman is arguably the most recognizable HBCU ever. On Instagram, only Howard University has more followers than the The Hillman Files, which serves as the school's unofficial IG account.

More than just a television show, *A Different World* represented a community where young viewers could see themselves in a myriad of characters. It shared with the world that Black people and HBCUs are not a monolith. Featuring a variety of socioeconomic, cultural, and educational differences was essential. Viewers saw characters like Dwayne Wayne, a tech genius on full scholarship; Whitley Gilbert, an affluent and occasionally tone-deaf debutante;

Ron Johnson, a super-senior in no hurry to graduate; Jaleesa Vincent, an older nontraditional student; Lena James, a student from the inner city with a lot of edge; and Freddie Brooks, a quirky hippie girl with a free spirit. The show also tried to dispel the myth that HBCUs enroll only Black students with the character of Maggie Lauten, a white girl who appeared a lot in the first season. Hillman provided viewers with a glimpse into the promise of college and allowed Black students to see themselves in a space not depicted elsewhere on television at that time. Hillman laid a foundation for understanding the extraordinary authenticity and potential that real HBCUs have.

While there are currently a lot of people and organizations highlighting HBCUs, no one person or entity does it like Vice President Kamala Harris, who is a proud Howard University alumna. She attributes a great deal of her success to the exposure she received to social justice activism, to becoming a member of Alpha Kappa Alpha, and to just being in a place like "Chocolate City" in those formative years.

> "At an HBCU, a young person is shown they can be anything. You
> step out of the minority and you become the majority. Everything
> tells you exactly what Aretha told us: You are young, gifted,
> and Black, you come as you are and leave as you aspire to be."
> (US Vice President Kamala Harris)

Stacey Abrams and Senator Raphael Warnock are political game-changers who attended Spelman and Morehouse, respectively. Not only did they change the political landscape in the state of Georgia, they also helped shape how elections will look moving forward. And then there is Michael Strahan, Super Bowl champion, a perennial Pro Bowl player, and successful entrepreneur, who now wakes up the nation on *Good Morning America* and who graduated from Texas Southern University. While these four individuals make a major impact, the groundswell of HBCUs' resurgence is much larger.

Beyoncé's 2018 Netflix special *Homecoming* paid homage to HBCU culture; Netflix CEO Reed Hastings and his wife, Patty Quillin, have donated millions to HBCUs, as has philanthropist MacKenzie Scott, along with several corporations; the 2021 NBA All-Star Game celebrated and donated millions to HBCUs; Coach Deion Sanders served as the head football coach at Jackson State University before leaving for the University of Colorado at Boulder; and recently basketball great LeBron James arranged to have his logo featured on Florida A&M's basketball jerseys. These are some of the notable people and events that have helped train a spotlight on these storied and necessary institutions.

University of Colorado (PWI)
Boulder, CO
29,000 Undergraduates
Public
Graduate Students: Yes
Setting: Suburban

Currently there are a little more than one hundred HBCUs. This is significantly fewer than there were fifty years ago. According to the United Negro College Fund, HBCUs make up only 3 percent of the country's colleges and universities, yet they enroll 10 percent of all Black students and produce almost 20 percent of all Black college graduates. While this number is impressive, the percentage of Black students who received their degrees from HBCUs prior to desegregation was far larger. These institutions were responsible for granting more than 90 percent of the college degrees earned by Blacks prior to desegregation. HBCUs are still responsible, though, for producing the majority of Black doctors, PhDs, federal judges, attorneys, military officers, and other professionals. With such a long history of success, why are HBCUs often overlooked in favor of PWIs by both families and school counselors in the college admissions process? Some Black families have a hard time seeing HBCUs as viable options for their children. One college counselor explains:

> "A lot of Black families who did not attend HBCUs or have some kind of connection to an HBCU have a hard time considering them as viable options because they are uncertain if they have the value and appeal in comparison to PWIs." (Independent school college counselor)

For the better part of sixty years since desegregation in the United States, there was a shift of high-profile Black talent from HBCUs to PWIs. Today, though, with a lot of attention given to social justice issues and the Black Lives Matter movement, along with growing interest in philanthropic giving to HBCUs, these schools are enjoying a resurgence of the popularity and significance they had in the early 1990s, when many hip-hop artists wore HBCU clothing in their music videos. This deliberate fashion statement was a staple in popular television shows and movies such as *Martin*, *The Cosby Show*, *A Different World*, *Boyz n the Hood*, and *School Daze*. While great producers and filmmakers like John Singleton (University of Southern California) and Spike Lee led the charge in the 1990s, there is a current resurgence led by Florida A&M alumnus William Packer, who has helped reignite this tradition of highlighting HBCUs in television and in cinema with several great movies featuring HBCU graduates Taraji P. Henson (Howard) and Terrence J (North Carolina A&T). Packer became the first Black producer of the Oscars in 2022, the same year Wanda Sykes (Hampton University) was a cohost.

University of Southern California (PWI)
Los Angeles, CA
21,000 Undergraduates
Private
Graduate Students: Yes
Setting: Urban

Florida A&M University (HBCU)
Tallahassee, FL
7,400 Undergraduates
Public
Graduate Students: Yes
Setting: Midsize City

North Carolina A&T State University (HBCU)
Greensboro, NC
11,000 Undergraduates
Public
Graduate Students: Yes
Setting: Midsize City

The Unmasking of Being Black in America

While many would like to think that George Floyd's death in 2020 at the hands of a police officer was an isolated incident, it wasn't. The deaths of Breonna Taylor, Eric Garner, Philando Castile, Daunte Wright, and so many other Black people have brought greater attention to a growing tension in race relations that has been building for years. While police brutality was nothing new, the graphic nature of the video that captured Derek Chauvin casually kneeling on the neck of George Floyd made it very real to all that much needed to be done in support of Black Lives Matter to address the hundreds of years of racial oppression that has affected so many parts of the Black experience in the United States, especially when it comes to economics and education.

From November 2016 through January 2021, America was exposed as being at a cultural crossroads during the reign of a tyrant in the White House who intentionally and blatantly divided our nation more than other presidents in recent memory. The effects of his presidency prompted a showdown of racism to a magnitude that we have not seen in decades in our society and planted seeds of divisiveness that continue to sprout across the country. One outgrowth of this division is a campaign to alter critical elements of Black American history—such as slavery and segregation—as they are taught in the curricula of public schools. In addition, there have been numerous cases of Black students who attend predominantly white high schools taking to social media to document painful incidents of racism they experienced at school. Many of the stories and Instagram pages attracted national news, especially since many of these instances took place at some of the country's top private and independent schools.

> "Almost every day at my school the white guys in my class ask me for the n-word pass. I feel offended every time, but I gave in to them because of the pressure. I feel like they won't like me if I don't give it to them. Now they say it to me all the time, more than I hear it from my Black friends in my neighborhood. I regret giving them the pass every day, but that is how the boys at my school are. I regret ever going to my school." (Student at a private school in Atlanta, June 22, 2020)

> "One day at lunch I asked one of my white peers to throw my cup away because he was next to the trash can. I joked and said, 'do it

*if Black Lives Matter.' He then said, 'Black lives don't matter' and
proceeded to kick my cup. Everyone around him applauded and
laughed at me."* (Student at a private school in Washington,
DC, September 15, 2020)

*"When President Obama was elected, we had a school wide assembly
to watch his inauguration. I'll never forget sitting in that pew, watching him put his hand on the Bible, and hearing a guy in my grade
next to me say, 'I can't wait until this (n-word) gets assassinated.'"*
(Student at a private school in Chicago, July 1, 2020)

Given these experiences of isolation and hostility, some students
and families that would have never looked at HBCUs are now looking to these schools as places of refuge and acceptance. In addition
to high schoolers taking to social media, lots of students on PWI
campuses chimed in with their experiences as well, and some of
them decided to transfer to HBCUs.

Do It for the Culture

In 2018 Beyoncé was set to headline onstage at Coachella. She had
taken time off from her music career while she was pregnant and
spending time with her young children. Her long-awaited return to
the stage caused a great deal of excitement. Many were expecting
her to give an unforgettable performance, but I don't know if anyone
was expecting *Homecoming*. It was deeply rooted in HBCU culture;
it exuded the feel of HBCU football games and traditions—big band
sounds and dance and step teams. Those familiar with HBCU culture were well acquainted with everything about the performance,
but to many it was an introduction to football Saturdays at an
HBCU. Beyoncé did not attend an HBCU, but her father, Mathew
Knowles, attended Fisk University in Tennessee, and her upbringing
in Houston was steeped in the HBCU culture of Texas Southern
and nearby Prairie View A&M. Beyoncé is the biggest celebrity in

the world, and for her to use her platform to showcase HBCUs and their culture, and to include HBCUs in the creative process, helped to elevate these great schools.

While Beyoncé is one of the artists that helped put Houston on the map as it relates to music, fellow Houstonian Megan Jovon Ruth Pete, also known as "Megan Thee Stallion," is doing all she can to keep Houston a focal part of the music world and highlight HBCUs as well. As she has risen to great fame in her hip-hop career, she also wanted to keep a promise to her family that she would finish school. In the winter of 2021, she fulfilled that promise when she graduated from Texas Southern University with a degree in health administration. While it's a great accomplishment for any student to complete their college degree, for a young person with everything to make that commitment goes a long way in promoting the value of a college education. That's "doing it for the culture!"

Fisk University (HBCU)
Nashville, TN
900 Undergraduates
Private
Graduate Students: Yes
Setting: Urban

Texas Southern University (HBCU)
Houston, TX
5,300 Undergraduates
Public
Graduate Students: Yes
Setting: Urban

Prairie View A&M University (HBCU)
Prairie View, TX
8,400 Undergraduates
Public
Graduate Students: Yes
Setting: Remote

Just as Beyoncé used her giant platform to shine a light on HBCUs, NBA star Chris Paul, the "official" HBCU ambassador, has used the NBA global stage and social media to champion HBCUs. The 2021 NBA All-Star Game was a collective effort by the association's players to bring attention to social justice efforts, but there is no doubt that Chris Paul's passion for Black colleges has heightened the attention. Although he attended a PWI, Wake Forest University, to play college basketball, Chris Paul has supported HBCUs throughout his life and all-star career, so much so that he recently completed his bachelor's degree from Winston-Salem State University. He is a native of North Carolina, which is home to several prominent HBCUs. He often wears clothing featuring the names of HBCUs to nationally televised games, and he wore Support Black Colleges–branded clothing in commercials for State Farm Insurance. In November 2021, he hosted the inaugural Chris Paul Classic, which is a two-day doubleheader with Morehouse College, Virginia Union University, West Virginia State University, and Winston-Salem State University.

Fellow NBA all-star Stephen Curry also recently went back to finish his undergraduate degree—his from Davidson College. Like Paul, he too has championed HBCUs. Curry has donated funds to Howard University's golf program for multiple years. This investment has led to Howard having a leading Division I golf program. When superstars like Curry and Paul return to college to earn their degree, that speaks loudly to their commitment to college education, as does their backing of HBCU athletic programs.

Chris Paul recently brought attention to Winston-Salem State University, yet longtime journalist and fellow WSSU alumnus Stephen A. Smith, cohost of ESPN's *First Take*, has been making the school proud for decades with his award-winning work with the NBA and other professional sports. In 2023 Smith joined forces with Shannon Sharpe, a Savannah State University alumnus and member of the NFL's Hall of Fame, to raise *First Take* to the next level by making it the first major sports talk show to be led by two HBCU graduates.

Wake Forest University (PWI)
Winston-Salem, NC
5,200 Undergraduate
Private
Graduate Students: Yes
Setting: Midsize City

Winston-Salem State University (HBCU)
Winston-Salem, NC
4,700 Undergraduate
Public
Graduate Students: Yes
Setting: Midsize City

Virginia Union University (HBCU)
Richmond, VA
1,200 Undergraduates
Private
Graduate Students: Yes
Setting: Midsize City

West Virginia State University (HBCU)
Institute, WV
3,500 Undergraduate Students
Public
Graduate Students: Yes
Setting: Suburban

Davidson College (PWI)
Davidson, NC
1,900 Undergraduates
Private
Graduate Students: No
Setting: Suburban

Another high-profile athlete who brought both his celebrity and talent to promoting HBCUs is Coach Deion "Prime Time" Sanders, who attended Florida State University but graduated from Talladega College in Alabama. His acceptance of the head coach position at Jackson State University in Mississippi, prior to his moving on to the University of Colorado, brought great attention to the school and its athletic program. During the two full seasons he was there, he made a major impact on attracting talent by signing some of the nation's top four- and five-star recruits, who in previous recruiting cycles would have considered larger, better-known programs. This movement of top talent to HBCUs is not limited to football. Other top athletes have decided to forgo larger athletic programs for the Black college experience. There are other NFL greats—Eddie George, who attended a PWI, Ohio State University, took the head coach job at Tennessee State University, and former NFL head coach Hue Jackson went to Grambling State University—leading football programs at HBCUs. These coaches did not attend an HBCU themselves, but by using their celebrity to bring attention to HBCUs, they are attracting the notice of prospective students and athletes, as well as major donors and corporate sponsors.

Florida State University (PWI)
Tallahassee, FL
30,000 Undergraduates
Public
Graduate Students: Yes
Setting: Midsize City

Jackson State University (HBCU)
Jackson, MS
4,700 Undergraduates
Public
Graduate Students: Yes
Setting: Midsize City

Ohio State University (PWI)
Columbus, OH
54,000 Undergraduates
Public
Graduate Students: Yes
Setting: Urban

Grambling State University (HBCU)
Grambling, LA
4,500 Undergraduates
Public
Graduate Students: Yes
Setting: Remote

In spring 2022, clothing company Ralph Lauren announced an upcoming limited-edition collection dedicated to Morehouse and Spelman. With designs by a Morehouse alumnus, James Jeter, the collaboration represents another elevation of HBCU culture, and Jeter and Ralph Lauren should be saluted for this endeavor.

A New Culture of Giving

One of the biggest challenges that HBCUs have always faced is a shortage of funding. This is probably the biggest reason for the decrease in the number of HBCUs. Both HBCUs and PWIs suffer from minimal giving from their alumni bases, which means that many schools are dependent on state and federal funds, external generated revenue, research funding, tuition revenue, and gifts from major individual and corporate donors. Consequently, most higher education institutions operate on tight budgets. In 2017, alumni giving accounted for only 26 percent of all educational donations.

Some may wonder why schools do not use their endowments to fund their operations, but the reality is that colleges and universities try to build up their endowments, not pull from them. Endowments are often a source of schools' fiscal strength and prestige. There are some HBCUs with sizable endowments, but most HBCUs' endowments are dwarfed by those of some of the nation's oldest universities. To give a sense of the funding disparity, Harvard's endowment is over $50 billion, whereas the largest HBCU endowment, Howard University's, is just over $850 million, followed by Spelman, which has just under $600 million in its endowment. With these great disparities in institutional resources, financial support for HBCUs is critical. Although hundreds of millions of dollars have poured into a small number of HBCUs in the past couple of years, there are so many more schools that need assistance.

The onset of the COVID-19 pandemic in 2020 produced fiscal challenges for all industries. In higher education, institutions had to conduct classes virtually and were not able to house students on campus or host summer camps, which are both large revenue generators for small institutions. Although the pandemic's effects are still being felt in higher education, there recently were record numbers of major gifts for several HBCUs. These generous gifts helped to reestablish the ambitious missions of HBCUs and provided exposure to some of the lesser-known schools. These gifts also inspired corporations such as MasterCard, Home Depot, Federal Express, Dominion Energy, and others to donate and create programs to support students at HBCUs.

Although these generous gifts were celebrated, many familiar with philanthropy would argue that it was the gift from Robert F. Smith to Morehouse College graduates that was the most impactful. In 2019 he pledged to pay off over $34 million in student loans for the graduating class. Mr. Smith is not a Morehouse alum (he attended Cornell University), but his gift was announced as he spoke at commencement. The story dominated national news for days following. Robert Smith, Reed Hastings (Bowdoin College), Michael R. Bloomberg (Johns Hopkins University), and MacKenzie Scott (Princeton University) are not the only people who have given to HBCUs, of course. We would be remiss if we did not remark that Oprah Winfrey has been giving to HBCUs for decades, along with many other organizations and individuals committed to HBCUs and their success led by the United Negro College Fund; however, the size of these recent gifts along with their timing is a major reason for a newfound interest in HBCUs.

Cornell University (PWI)
Ithaca, NY
15,000 Undergraduates
Private
Graduate Students: Yes
Setting: Midsize City

Bowdoin College (PWI)
Brunswick, ME
1,800 Undergraduates
Private
Graduate Students: No
Setting: Remote

Johns Hopkins University (PWI)
Baltimore, MD
5,300 Undergraduates
Private
Graduate Students: Yes
Setting: Urban

In addition to increased private and corporate philanthropy for HBCUs of late, the Biden-Harris administration has allocated more than $5.8 billion to the support of Black colleges. The administration appointed Taraji P. Henson and Chris Paul to its HBCU advisory board. The board is led by Drs. Tony Allen (president of Delaware State) and Glenda Glover (outgoing president of Tennessee State). Dr. Dietra Trent was appointed the executive director of the White House's HBCU initiative.

The fact that HBCUs are responsible for producing 80 percent of Black judges, 85 percent of Black doctors, and 50 percent of Black lawyers, as well as the majority of Black PhDs, should say a lot in their favor. One could make the argument that PWIs are more diverse in their makeup of students, but in terms of producing Black professionals, HBCUs do more than their PWI counterparts.

Also deserving of mention is Robert Mason, founder of the Common Black College Application. A proud graduate of Virginia State University, Mason created a platform that allows students to apply to any number of more than fifty HBCUs for only twenty dollars. This tool has simplified the college application process for many families, while promoting HBCUs and college access. Mason's platform has contributed to the current increase of attention paid to HBCUs.

Virginia State University (HBCU)
Petersburg, VA
4,300 Undergraduates
Public
Graduate Students: Yes
Setting: Remote

When top national recruits decide to attend HBCU programs over Power Five conferences (SEC, ACC, Big 12, Pac-12, Big Ten), it becomes a big deal and makes national headlines, as does Beyoncé taking the stage at Coachella and Ralph Lauren curating a clothing collection; both are sharing Black college culture and fashion with the world. These events have led to increased recognition and fund-raising from philanthropic leaders and corporations. Given the current cultural climate in the country, along with the challenges that many Black students face in education systems, we highly recommend that all Black parents, HBCU alums or not, educate themselves about the historical and current relevance of HBCUs and then encourage their children to consider them to be valuable and viable educational options.

CHAPTER 4

The Power 3
(The Black Ivies)

Overview

There is a best, a top tier, an elite in all industries and professions. HBCUs are no different, and for decades three schools have been leaders in the world of HBCUs. Howard, Spelman, and Morehouse are undeniably the most famous HBCUs, given their long lists of famous alumni and the thousands of other graduates who are committed to serving the world and praising these proud institutions. There are those who attended other great HBCUs (insert the name of your HBCU here: _____) who will take issue with this assertion; however, this chapter is not meant as a slight to any of those other institutions.

This chapter serves as an introduction to the greatness of HBCUs, with Spelman, Howard, and Morehouse serving as proxies for the many other great ones around the country. Just as most people declare that PWIs have a top three with Harvard, Princeton, and Yale, the same argument can be made for these three HBCUs. While some will not agree with this chapter's title, the goal of the chapter is to move the conversation beyond these three schools for Black families looking for great schools and for guidance counselors looking for recommendations among the more than one hundred HBCUs.

The argument over who or what is the best happens in social spaces throughout society. Among Black people it happens in beauty salons and barbershops, over spades games and at family reunions and cookouts, on any number of subjects. If you want to get a heated conversation going, just ask a question that begins, "What/Who is the best . . . ?" While many of these conversations are highly subjective, in most instances there is some agreement about the top picks in whatever category you are discussing. For instance, if someone were to ask who is the best basketball player of all time, for which there is no real argument in our opinion, we would say Michael Jordan (University of North Carolina, Chapel Hill), but there are others who would say LeBron James, Magic Johnson (Michigan State University), Kareem Abdul-Jabbar (University of California, Los Angeles), or maybe Wilt Chamberlain (University of Kansas). Still, the list is short when talking about the best. Similarly, if someone were to ask about the top Black movies, you would hear titles like *Love Jones*, *The Color Purple*, and *Coming to America* but would likely not hear *Soul Plane*. As hard as it may be to acknowledge, some hierarchies shape the lens through which we see life. Hierarchy is certainly one of the biggest concerns in the college admissions process. Many people focus on the rankings of about one hundred colleges and universities, when in fact there are some four thousand colleges and universities across the country.

University of North Carolina at Chapel Hill (PWI)
Chapel Hill, NC
18,000 Undergraduates
Public
Graduate Students: Yes
Setting: Midsize City

Michigan State University (PWI)
Lansing, MI
35,000 Undergraduates
Public
Graduate Students: Yes
Setting: Midsize City

University of California at Los Angeles (PWI)
Los Angeles, CA
30,000 Undergraduates
Public
Graduate Students: Yes
Setting: Urban

University of Kansas (PWI)
Lawrence, KS
35,000 Undergraduates
Public
Graduate Students: Yes
Setting: Midsize City

As we wrote this book, we reflected on the many names in Black America that serve as the standards of inspiration and leadership; the names that immediately came to mind were Congressman John Lewis, Vice President Kamala Harris, Dr. Martin Luther King Jr., Reverend Jesse Jackson, President Barack Obama, and Justice Thurgood Marshall—all with the exception of President Obama were graduates of HBCUs. While there are Black success stories and graduates from all higher education institutions, many of the names that defined Black success in the twentieth century and are defining success in the twenty-first century are HBCU graduates, and most of them had some direct or indirect connection to Howard, Morehouse, or Spelman.

Howard, Morehouse, and Spelman arguably have the greatest sets of distinguished alumni of any schools in the country, Black or white. Of course, there are other HBCUs with distinguished alumni such as Tennessee State, where Oprah Winfrey went; Lincoln University, where Langston Hughes and Thurgood Marshall attended; and Grambling State, where Doug Williams went and later became the first Black quarterback to win the Super Bowl, just to name a few.

> Should these three schools be the only HBCUs your child considers? Do they have everything your child needs? Is our statement about prestige unfair to other HBCUs and their history and efforts?

Spelman

In many college rankings, there is no HBCU ranked higher than Spelman College. Spelman has secured its position as the top HBCU in the country for years. And if you meet a Spelman graduate, she will surely tell you why or be "undaunted" by you not agreeing. Since its founding in 1881, Spelman has been the leader in educating Black women to accomplish great things and to commit their lives to service. As a liberal arts school, much like its brother school Morehouse, Spelman's primary aim is to prepare its graduates to be leaders in their chosen vocation. There is an expectation that Spelman women will shine their light on the world and boldly claim that their alma mater is part of the reason they are so powerful.

If you are looking for a name that speaks to the best of Spelman, you need look no farther than political powerhouse Stacey Abrams, class of 1995. Her grassroots organization Fair Fight created voter awareness and fought voter suppression leading up to the 2020 election, and it provided a network to change the senate makeup in Georgia. Spelman's place among the top HBCUs is not due solely to its name recognition but also to its track record for producing top doctors, lawyers, and leaders in all industries. Its list of graduates includes Rosalind Brewer, who until recently served as the CEO of Walgreens and was one of only two Black women serving as the CEO of Fortune 500 companies. Prior to taking her leadership role at Walgreens, Brewer served as the COO of Starbucks. The other is Thasunda Brown Duckett, the CEO of TIAA, who attended the University of Houston.

University of Houston (PWI)
Houston, TX
38,000 Undergraduates
Public
Graduate Students: Yes
Setting: Urban

The recently coined "Black Girl Magic" names a movement where Black women empower other Black women and see one another as supportive and inspirational. As Black people, our children need to be pushed to excellence, first by us and then by their peers. This happens at Spelman, and it's why every brilliant Black girl needs to learn more about Spelman before she makes a college decision. Spelman will not be for everyone, but given its history of producing some of the most accomplished Black women ever in the arts, medicine, business, academics, and politics, why wouldn't you consider it? Many Spelman women tell stories of their other college options, including admission to Ivy League schools. They made the decision not to attend these other schools because they wanted an HBCU experience, had concerns about the social environment of a PWI, or wanted to be surrounded by the power of other Black women. Clearly, Spelman women are in a class by themselves.

It is hard for us as Black men to rank one school over another if they are all serving Black people well, but we know there are hierarchies with "better" and "best." Spelman is the best, has produced the best, and expects to be the best. Your daughter must be a superlative student to get into Spelman and have access to its exclusive community. The school admits less than 40 percent of its applicants and expects them to have a grade point average (GPA) above 3.8, an SAT score above 1200, and a score between 27 and 30 on the ACT. And that is just to start. Young women must also have demonstrated a commitment to service and have established themselves as leaders who want to contribute to society. High school students who want to attend Spelman are usually near the top of their graduating class, have taken advanced coursework (Advanced Placement or International Baccalaureate courses), have extensive extracurricular activities, and have written a personal essay that reveals what's most important to them about the next stage of their educational journey. Simply put, applicants to Spelman need to work before they play, understanding that their social life comes secondary to their scholarly aspirations.

Morehouse

Morehouse stands alone as the premier all-men's HBCU, not only because it's the only one, but also because of the kinds of young men it attracts and nurtures. Morehouse men are intent on their goals. College is not a playground but rather is the first step of their life's ascension. As we discuss in chapter 10, we understand that college-educated Black men are, unfortunately, an endangered species. For multiple reasons, we are a serious minority on PWI campuses and on co-ed HBCU campuses as well. A recent statistic cited for most HBCU campuses is a ratio of women to men of seven to one. The Atlanta University Center, which consists of Morehouse, Spelman, and Clark Atlanta University, has a male to female ratio of nine to one. This suggests that Black men have not been given the same educational foundation or have not taken as much advantage of educational opportunities as others have; thus they need a place dedicated to their development. Morehouse is that place.

When it comes to Morehouse, the name of one of its graduates must be mentioned: Dr. Martin Luther King Jr. His legacy as a scholar and civil rights leader has helped define how the world sees Morehouse and has helped shape many graduates who walk in his footsteps, such as Raphael Warnock, class of 1991, who is currently serving in the US Senate. Like Dr. King, he too served as a minister at Ebenezer Baptist Church. While Dr. King is the gold standard of Morehouse graduates, Morehouse College has no shortage of impressive alumni, including Olympic gold medalist Edwin Moses, Academy Award winners Samuel L. Jackson and Spike Lee, civil rights leader Julian Bond, late businessman Herman Cain, and Congressman Cedric Richmond, who is currently serving as a senior advisor in the Biden administration. These accomplished alumni exemplify Morehouse's long track record of graduating leaders across all fields. These alumni have inspired a new generation of Morehouse leaders: Randall Woodfin, mayor of Birmingham, Alabama, who was elected to his second term; and Steven Reed, mayor of Montgomery, Alabama, who is the first African American to hold that position, just to name a few.

Founded in 1867, Morehouse started as and still is the largest all-men's liberal arts college in the country. With only 2,100 men on campus, it prides itself on community, professionalism, and social justice. Legions of men attribute their success and how they approach life to their Morehouse education. It stands alone as *the* college where men are formed for service. Much like Spelman, admission is competitive. Only about six hundred matriculate every year. The expected GPA of an applicant to Morehouse is 3.5, with scores of 1000 on the SAT and between 20 and 25 on the ACT. These might not be earth-shattering statistics for Black students who expect to go to Harvard, Princeton, or Yale, but they are more than solid and are a testament to Morehouse not being measured by whom it admits but by whom it graduates. Men of distinction. Men of character. Men of courage. Morehouse men set themselves apart by understanding that they represent more than just themselves; they also represent their families and the history of their institution.

Samuel L. Jackson has acted in films that collectively have grossed more than $27 billion worldwide, making him the highest-grossing actor of all time.

If you have a Black male child whom you wish to make an impact on the world, please consider Morehouse.

The combination of "Spelhouse" is a powerful network of Black excellence. It truly is a family where people understand and appreciate one another. For your child even to consider one of these schools is a privilege, and to attend would be an honor.

Howard

Howard University is called "The Mecca" for a reason. There is a spiritual, euphoric element about being on the campus where so much Black excellence began its journey. While we have already listed the names of its graduates that most Americans know, there are others: award-winning author Ta-Nehisi Coates, former mayor and US ambassador Andrew Young, attorney and the late businessman Vernon Jordan, and Kamilah Forbes, executive producer of the Apollo Theater and an acclaimed filmmaker. Even Tim's sister attended Howard! These illustrious graduates prove that Howard has and continues to influence all aspects of art, politics, and American culture.

Why is Howard so highly regarded? It's because of its history, location, academic resources, professional schools, and homecoming. In almost every ranking among well-traveled Black folks who have gone to homecomings, Howard is declared to have *the* best homecoming celebration of any HBCU. (I, Tim, don't agree, nor does North Carolina A&T, which trademarked its homecoming the "Greatest Homecoming on Earth," or GHOE.)

We're not here to argue or compare, so instead let us simply share why your child should aspire to be a Howard Bison. If your child has gifts in science and is considering medical school, Howard prepares students well. What about business? Howard has a business school dedicated to the study of finance, marketing, and accounting. Does your child want to study communications and aspires to be a journalist or to work in public relations? Howard has that too. And if your child aspires to go into public service or law, Howard has established itself as one of the best.

The beauty of Howard is that there is something for everyone, and we have not even mentioned its recently renamed Chadwick Boseman School of Fine Arts, where dancer and actress Debbie Allen excelled and where her equally accomplished sister, Phylicia Rashad, is now the dean of the school. Other notable artists that attended Howard are Zora Neale Hurston, Donny Hathaway, Eric Roberson, Taraji P. Henson, Susan Kelechi Watson, and Sean "Diddy" Combs. Nestled in northwest Washington, DC, Howard plays a special role in the politics of the US government. Its proximity to power makes it an ideal place for internships.

To be admitted to Howard, your child must be a scholar. Howard accepts less than 30 percent of applicants, and its GPA and ACT and SAT expectations are higher than Morehouse's and Spelman's. Howard looks for students who are ready to excel in specific disciplines; hence it has the specialized schools of a research university as opposed to being a liberal arts college.

Beyond Spelman, Morehouse, and Howard being household names, they also have what real estate developers value most: location, location. When you think of cities with a history of Black cultural relevance, Atlanta and Washington, DC, are at the top of the list. The foundation of the civil rights movement was formed in Atlanta, and some of the greatest gatherings of Blacks occurred in the District of Columbia: March on Washington, Million Man March, and the inauguration of Barack Obama. Both of these cities have witnessed Black success in so many ways, which makes them great destinations for college and opportunity. In addition to opportunities for internships and conducting research, these locations provide great access to social activities and public transportation. Students can explore and enjoy these great cities as a complement to their college education.

I (Tim) would add that these cities and schools offer what some would call a "safe" space. While many will maintain that there are very few safe spaces for Blacks in this country, HBCUs might be the ideal location for Black students to have their college experience. As an HBCU graduate, I have often wondered why so many Black students apply only to PWIs and then arrive on campus and want more faculty of color, support systems for underrepresented students, and more diversity. But when asked why they did not apply to an HBCU, they say that they or their parents never considered it. I often ask myself why we as Blacks are so insistent on putting ourselves in spaces that are not made for us. Why should we have to alter who we are and how we conduct ourselves to fit in? We have the safe spaces of Morehouse, Spelman, Howard, and other HBCUs that allow us just to be, places where we are surrounded by people who resemble us and nurture us inside and outside the classroom. Our safety and the uplifting of our culture should be a priority for us regardless of whether we favor PWIs or HBCUs.

We profiled Spelman, Morehouse, and Howard to start a conversation about Black colleges, not to put them above other HBCUs. We drew a parallel to Harvard, Princeton, and Yale, which many consider the top PWIs for many of the same reasons we have put forth. People will always want to know what or who is the best; it is just human nature, and we happen to be talking about colleges. Beyond Howard, Morehouse, and Spelman, there are other great HBCUs like Florida A&M, Hampton, North Carolina A&T, Morgan State, Fisk, and Xavier University of Louisiana, which all have histories of producing leaders in all professions. (Please, alums from the other ninety-plus HBCUs, don't come for us!)

Hampton University (HBCU)
Hampton, VA
3,100 Undergraduates
Private
Graduate Students: Yes
Setting: Midsize City

Morgan State University (HBCU)
Baltimore, MD
6,300 Undergraduates
Public
Graduate Students: Yes
Setting: Urban

Xavier University of Louisiana (HBCU)
New Orleans, LA
2,500 Undergraduates
Private
Graduate Students: Yes
Setting: Urban

Accredited HBCUs by State

Name	State	Type	Campus setting	Campus housing	Undergraduate students
Alabama A&M University	Alabama	4-year, public	Midsize city	Yes	5,093
Alabama State University	Alabama	4-year, public	Midsize city	Yes	3,614
Bishop State Community College	Alabama	2-year, public	Midsize city	No	2,176
Gadsden State Community College	Alabama	2-year, public	Small city	Yes	3,993
H. Councill Trenholm State Community College	Alabama	2-year, public	Midsize city	No	1,526
J. F. Drake State Community and Technical College	Alabama	2-year, public	Midsize city	No	825
Lawson State Community College	Alabama	2-year, public	Midsize city	Yes	2,823
Miles College	Alabama	4-year, private nonprofit	Small suburb	Yes	1,440
Oakwood University	Alabama	4-year, private nonprofit	Midsize city	Yes	1,339
Shelton State Community College	Alabama	2-year, public	Midsize city	No	3,743
Stillman College	Alabama	4-year, private nonprofit	Midsize city	Yes	712
Talladega College	Alabama	4-year, private nonprofit	Remote town	Yes	1,142

Name	State	Type	Campus setting	Campus housing	Undergraduate students
Tuskegee University	Alabama	4-year, private nonprofit	Remote town	Yes	2,280
Arkansas Baptist College	Arkansas	4-year, primarily associate's degrees, private nonprofit	Midsize city	Yes	468
Philander Smith College	Arkansas	4-year, private nonprofit	Midsize city	Yes	799
Shorter College	Arkansas	2-year, private nonprofit	Small city	No	223
University of Arkansas at Pine Bluff	Arkansas	4-year, public	Small city	Yes	2,507
Delaware State University	Delaware	4-year, public	Small city	Yes	4,131
Bethune-Cookman University	Florida	4-year, private nonprofit	Small city	Yes	2,746
Edward Waters College	Florida	4-year, private nonprofit	Large city	Yes	2,273
Florida A&M University	Florida	4-year, public	Midsize city	Yes	7,402
Florida Memorial University	Florida	4-year, private nonprofit	Large suburb	Yes	887
Albany State University	Georgia	4-year, public	Small city	Yes	6,102
Clark Atlanta University	Georgia	4-year, private nonprofit	Large city	Yes	3,096
Fort Valley State University	Georgia	4-year, public	Remote town	Yes	2,794

(continued)

Accredited HBCUs by State (*continued*)

Name	State	Type	Campus setting	Campus housing	Undergraduate students
Interdenominational Theological Center	Georgia	4-year, private nonprofit	Large city	Yes	None; graduate school
Morehouse College	Georgia	4-year, private nonprofit	Large city	Yes	2,152
Morehouse School of Medicine	Georgia	4-year, private nonprofit	Large city	No	None; graduate school
Morris Brown College	Georgia	4-year, private nonprofit	Large city	Yes	400
Paine College	Georgia	4-year, private nonprofit	Midsize city	Yes	189
Savannah State University	Georgia	4-year, public	Midsize city	Yes	3,245
Spelman College	Georgia	4-year, private nonprofit	Large city	Yes	2,207
Kentucky State University	Kentucky	4-year, public	Remote town	Yes	2,148
Simmons College of Kentucky	Kentucky	4-year, private nonprofit	Large city	No	140
Dillard University	Louisiana	4-year, private nonprofit	Large city	Yes	1,215
Grambling State University	Louisiana	4-year, public	Remote town	Yes	4,511
Southern University and A&M College	Louisiana	4-year, public	Midsize city	Yes	6,145
Southern University at New Orleans	Louisiana	4-year, public	Large city	Yes	1,941

Name	State	Type	Campus setting	Campus housing	Undergraduate students
Southern University at Shreveport	Louisiana	2-year, public	Midsize city	Yes	3,013
Southern University Law Center	Louisiana	4-year, public	Midsize city	No	None; graduate school
Xavier University of Louisiana	Louisiana	4-year, private nonprofit	Large city	Yes	2,517
Bowie State University	Maryland	4-year, public	Large suburb	Yes	5,354
Coppin State University	Maryland	4-year, public	Large city	Yes	2,108
Morgan State University	Maryland	4-year, public	Large city	Yes	6,270
University of Maryland Eastern Shore	Maryland	4-year, public	Remote town	Yes	2,069
Alcorn State University	Mississippi	4-year, public	Remote town	Yes	2,729
Coahoma Community College	Mississippi	2-year, public	Remote town	Yes	1,612
Jackson State University	Mississippi	4-year, public	Midsize city	Yes	4,668
Mississippi Valley State University	Mississippi	4-year, public	Remote town	Yes	1,694
Rust College	Mississippi	4-year, private nonprofit	Remote town	Yes	623
Tougaloo College	Mississippi	4-year, private nonprofit	Midsize city	Yes	762

(continued)

Accredited HBCUs by State (*continued*)

Name	State	Type	Campus setting	Campus housing	Undergraduate students
Harris-Stowe State University	Missouri	4-year, public	Large city	Yes	1,400
Lincoln University of Missouri	Missouri	4-year, public	Small city	Yes	1,892
Bennett College	North Carolina	4-year, private nonprofit	Midsize city	Yes	232
Elizabeth City State University	North Carolina	4-year, public	Remote town	Yes	1,910
Fayetteville State University	North Carolina	4-year, public	Midsize city	Yes	5,661
Johnson C. Smith University	North Carolina	4-year, private nonprofit	Large city	Yes	1,253
Livingstone College	North Carolina	4-year, private nonprofit	Midsize suburb	Yes	845
North Carolina A&T State University	North Carolina	4-year, public	Midsize city	Yes	11,130
North Carolina Central University	North Carolina	4-year, public	Midsize city	Yes	6,067
Saint Augustine's University	North Carolina	4-year, private nonprofit	Large city	Yes	1,110
Shaw University	North Carolina	4-year, private nonprofit	Large city	Yes	1,152
Winston-Salem State University	North Carolina	4-year, public	Midsize city	Yes	4,689
Central State University	Ohio	4-year, public	Remote town	Yes	4,021
Wilberforce University	Ohio	4-year, private nonprofit	Remote town	Yes	439

Name	State	Type	Campus setting	Campus housing	Undergraduate students
Langston University	Oklahoma	4-year, public	Remote town	Yes	1,894
Cheyney University of Pennsylvania	Pennsylvania	4-year, public	Small suburb	Yes	623
Lincoln University	Pennsylvania	4-year, public	Remote town	Yes	1,895
Allen University	South Carolina	4-year, private nonprofit	Midsize city	Yes	656
Benedict College	South Carolina	4-year, private nonprofit	Midsize city	Yes	1,724
Claflin University	South Carolina	4-year, private nonprofit	Remote town	Yes	1,969
Clinton College	South Carolina	4-year, primarily associate's degrees, private nonprofit	Small city	Yes	119
Denmark Technical College	South Carolina	2-year, public	Remote town	Yes	491
Morris College	South Carolina	4-year, private nonprofit	Small city	Yes	395
South Carolina State University	South Carolina	4-year, public	Remote town	Yes	2,020
Voorhees College	South Carolina	4-year, private nonprofit	Remote town	Yes	368
American Baptist College	Tennessee	4-year, private nonprofit	Large city	Yes	55
Fisk University	Tennessee	4-year, private nonprofit	Large city	Yes	879
Lane College	Tennessee	4-year, private nonprofit	Small city	Yes	1,095

(continued)

Accredited HBCUs by State (*continued*)

Name	State	Type	Campus setting	Campus housing	Undergraduate students
LeMoyne-Owen College	Tennessee	4-year, private nonprofit	Large city	Yes	654
Meharry Medical College	Tennessee	4-year, private nonprofit	Large city	Yes	None; graduate school
Tennessee State University	Tennessee	4-year, public	Large city	Yes	6,000
Huston–Tillotson University	Texas	4-year, private nonprofit	Large city	Yes	1,045
Jarvis Christian College	Texas	4-year, private nonprofit	Remote town	Yes	719
Paul Quinn College	Texas	4-year, private nonprofit	Large city	Yes	468
Prairie View A&M University	Texas	4-year, public	Remote town	Yes	8,372
Southwestern Christian College	Texas	4-year, primarily associate's degrees, private nonprofit	Remote town	Yes	84
St. Philip's College	Texas	2-year, public	Large city	No	12,696
Texas College	Texas	4-year, private nonprofit	Midsize city	Yes	764
Texas Southern University	Texas	4-year, public	Large city	Yes	5,298
Wiley College	Texas	4-year, private nonprofit	Remote town	Yes	615
Hampton University	Virginia	4-year, private nonprofit	Midsize city	Yes	3,063

Name	State	Type	Campus setting	Campus housing	Undergraduate students
Norfolk State University	Virginia	4-year, public	Midsize city	Yes	4,992
Virginia State University	Virginia	4-year, public	Small city	Yes	3,659
Virginia Union University	Virginia	4-year, private nonprofit	Midsize city	Yes	1,209
Virginia University of Lynchburg	Virginia	4-year, primarily associate's degrees, private nonprofit	Small city	Yes	122
University of the Virgin Islands	Virgin Islands	4-year, public	Remote town	Yes	1,587
University of the Virgin Islands–Albert A. Sheen Campus	Virgin Islands	4-year, public	Remote town	Yes	546
Howard University	Washington, DC	4-year, private nonprofit	Large city	Yes	7,857
University of the District of Columbia	Washington, DC	4-year, public	Large city	No	3,385
University of the District of Columbia David A. Clarke School of Law	Washington, DC	4-year, public	Large city	No	None; graduate school
Bluefield State College	West Virginia	4-year, public	Remote town	No	1,243
West Virginia State University	West Virginia	4-year, public	Small suburb	Yes	3,502

CHAPTER 5

What Is a Liberal Arts Education, and Is It Worth It?

Overview

In this chapter, I (Shereem) will share my opinions about liberal arts education and how it prepares some people for anything and others for nothing. I ask: Is it worth it for our Black children? Too often I have seen students who were liberal arts majors struggle after graduation to find salaried jobs with high earning potential. This is where my primary frustration lies: In a world that equates success with money, are we doing ourselves and our children a disservice by not steering them toward an education that can lead to wealth generation?

This chapter was and still is my (Shereem's) baby. Provocative in nature, its claims were a point of contention in many presentations we gave on our book tour for the first edition. People who disagreed with me—which is fine—referred me to sources that have given me ample food for thought.

Most of my opponents come from a place of privilege and often have well-paying jobs. Without criticizing them or their opinions, I hope that our Black children who pursue any college degree— whether at a liberal arts, research-oriented, or pre-professional institution—will give some consideration to entrepreneurship. Why? Because within Black history, our greatest models of excellence have built mini-empires or used their gifts to serve our people. Oprah. Monique Nelson-Nwachuku. Black Wall Street. Dr. King. Jay-Z.

A liberal arts degree can be a great choice for aspiring entrepreneurs because it provides a well-rounded education that develops critical thinking, creativity, and problem-solving skills. These are essential qualities for any successful entrepreneur, as they enable someone to approach business challenges with an open mind. As an entrepreneur myself, I am a prime example of where lifelong learning, collaboration, effective communication, critical thinking, and adaptability can get you in life. This I cannot deny. And, for what it's worth, years of data collected from top business executives and hiring managers show that 80 percent of them agree that all students need a strong foundation in the liberal arts. Whoa. That's a big number.

Liberal arts degrees typically require students to take a broad sampling of courses in subjects like literature, philosophy, history, and the arts. This breadth of knowledge allows entrepreneurs to see the big picture and draw from a variety of sources when making decisions. In addition, a liberal arts degree instills a strong sense of curiosity and a desire to learn new things. This is crucial for entrepreneurship, as successful business owners are constantly seeking new opportunities, ideas, and knowledge to improve their businesses. They must also be able to adapt to changing market conditions and customer needs, which requires a willingness to experiment and take risks.

So what is my own stance—pro–liberal arts or pro-pre-professional? The rest of the chapter shines light on my leanings. Let me stress, though, that the purpose of this chapter is to help parents and students understand what a liberal arts education is so they can have productive discussions about possible majors when they are making plans for college.

In an ever-changing world, college degrees are no longer regarded as gateways to becoming middle or upper class as they once were. I'm sure some of us know someone who is frustrated with their profession and tends to blame it on their choice of major in college. Even more of us know someone who is not using their degree to its maximum potential. Many of us are still dancing with Sallie Mae, and we ask ourselves, "Was it worth it? Would I be farther ahead in life and wealth building if I were not saddled with educational debt?" And how many of us are in careers that are actually related to our college major?

Many college graduates, of all races, who majored in liberal arts question the monetary or professional value of their degrees. I am one of these people. Degrees in English, sociology, psychology, history, and the like are often undervalued, and in a global economy, without a graduate degree, some undergraduate degrees make many corporate employers question a person's capabilities. Worse than that, many liberal arts degrees suggest that graduates are not qualified to do anything with notable or predictable immediate earning power. There are exceptions, of course, and many of us are creative or entrepreneurial, which means that we may not have needed the degree.

As a liberal arts major (English and African American studies), I often found myself to be selectively employable and never for high-paying jobs that offered bonuses. As I have now witnessed a generation of my peers and mentored many students who have gone on to college, I think that college graduates with pre-professional degrees in business, engineering, computer science, nursing, information systems, architecture, communications, or other fields who are hired right out of college tend to fare better in the long term. Not having career and life direction stalls progress. I do not want this for my children or for yours.

What Is a Liberal Arts Education?

As defined by the Association of American Colleges and Universities, *liberal education* is an approach to undergraduate education that promotes the integration of learning across the curriculum and co-curriculum, and between academic and experiential learning, to develop specific learning outcomes that are essential for work, citizenship, and life. The *liberal arts* are a particular set of disciplines (the humanities, the arts, and the natural and social sciences). A *liberal arts college* is a type of higher education institution whose curriculum is designed to provide a liberal arts education. A liberal education includes the study of the liberal arts and is the approach undertaken at most liberal arts colleges, but it is not exclusive to those disciplines or to that institutional type.

Similarly, as defined by Princeton University—the alma mater of former First Lady Michelle Obama, Amazon's Jeff Bezos, and former CEO of BET, Bob Johnson—a liberal arts education offers an expansive intellectual grounding in all kinds of humanistic inquiry by having students explore issues, ideas, and methods across the humanities and the arts, and the natural and social sciences. These skills elevate conversations in the classroom and strengthen social and cultural analysis. They also let graduates navigate the world's most complex issues.

A liberal arts education challenges students to consider how to solve problems and trains them to determine which problems to solve and why, preparing them for positions of leadership and a life of service to the nation and all of humanity. Ultimately, a liberal arts education aims to help students "think outside the box."

Think about what?

Morehouse College is a liberal arts college just as Wesleyan University is a liberal arts university. These are the schools that Tim and I attended. Now here's the difference: beyond just teaching students how to think, Morehouse has a business major, a communication major, and specialty engineering majors. These are practical majors that lead to profitable careers. If college is supposed to educate as well as prepare our young people for professional success, we must commit to making sure that our Black children know how to earn money

Wesleyan University (PWI)
Middletown, CT
3,000 Undergraduates
Private
Graduate Students: Yes
Setting: Remote

once they graduate. Most of us—Black people—do not come from generational wealth. Thinking about how to get money or hoping to get money has kept too many Black people in economic despair. Sure, we're all waiting for the reparations they owe us for our ancestors, but in the meantime, for us, college is often seen as the first step toward a career and wealth building.

This is why I say *liberal arts is a luxury*. It's nice to learn how to think. It's nice to read books across multiple disciplines that encourage introspection and offer insights into other cultures, literatures, philosophies, and histories. It's advantageous to solve equations and collaborate with classmates on projects. So, I'm all for liberal arts if you can afford it. What I mean is that if you have no assurance that your child will get a job after graduation or has the ability to launch their own venture, they will probably need to go to graduate school to compete. So, I ask, who wants to pay for that? You? Or more loans?

I am a first-generation college student, and my father drove a UPS truck, making deliveries to get me through school. With his "good job" he was able to retire at fifty-five with a healthy pension. Because he had sent me to college, he assumed that I had learned how to invest and make money. Despite my being a teacher at the time, and his knowing I had an English degree, he once said to me, "Since you went to college, I want you to tell me where I should invest my money."

I had no clue what to tell him, and I was disappointed that I didn't know. I was never taught. Maybe he was supposed to teach me; maybe I was supposed to learn in high school or college. What I learned in that moment was that I had to teach myself. But I understood his assumption, and I think it's one we should all consider as Black parents: Is the point of college to get a diploma? Is it to expand our network and knowledge of the world? Is it a training ground to cultivate the capacity to make, keep, and grow money? Too often we think that all three are mutually exclusive, when, in fact, college ideally serves all the above.

The racial wealth gap is a long-standing issue that has plagued America for generations. Research shows that African Americans hold only 4 percent of the country's wealth, and the net worth of a white family is nearly ten times greater than that of a Black family. Aware of these staggering statistics, businessman and philanthropist Robert Smith—who pledged to pay all the student loan debt for the Morehouse class of 2019—and others are doing what they can to break down socioeconomic barriers standing in the way of Blacks generating wealth.

In our many interviews and roundtable discussions, we broached the topic of parents being supportive of their child choosing a liberal arts major that did not equip them to be employable at a satisfactory or predictable salary upon graduation. Most Black parents were clear that they want to and will support their children's choice of major. No one said that they were steering their children only toward making money. When I asked "why not?" the responses were not clear. Some did not want their child to feel pressured; others were convinced that money would come when the time is right. I agree with both sentiments. The harder issue is the accumulation of student and parent debt. With the cost of college being what it is today, how many of us are discussing how this education will be financed and by whom? How will the debt be repaid? My call to action is for us to discuss a plan with our children—for their majors, their possible careers, and, if necessary, their debt repayment.

"I do not want my child to be burdened with college loans long after graduation. One of the biggest mistakes I made was not having a steady income after college and repaying my loans immediately. I worked as a temp before I decided to go back for my master's because I was never a salaried employee. My undergraduate degree in psychology pretty much demanded that I go back to school, but now I had loans from undergrad and graduate school. I enjoyed studying psychology, and I have no regrets about my choice of major, but I do not want my son to have to struggle *after college the way I did. I'm forty-three and still paying off my loans."* (PWI graduate and parent)

Some of us exasperate our children by insisting they major in business or STEM (science, technology, engineering, and mathematics). We do it because we don't want them to struggle. We also do it because we want them to be part of a global community that primarily communicates through three ways: money, technology, and art. Remember that Jay-Z line from "Can't Knock the Hustle"? "All Blacks got is sports and entertainment." I remember hearing that line and cringing. I'm sure corporate business moguls Dick Parsons (University of Hawai'i at Mānoa), Kenneth Chenault (Bowdoin College), and others did too. But the truth hurts, and there is definitely brutal honesty in what Hov said. At the time, Bill Cosby (Temple University), Bob Johnson, L. A. Reid, Eddie Murphy, Michael Jordan, and Oprah Winfrey were the richest Black people that most of us knew. Sports and entertainment. Today, our most recognizable figures are LeBron James, Drake, Kevin Hart, Byron Allen (University of Southern California), Shonda Rhimes (Dartmouth College), and Serena Williams. Again, sports and entertainment. Beyoncé Knowles-Carter and Shawn Carter are known to be American royalty, and their success comes from . . . you already know. Thankfully the Obamas came along and made an exception to the rule, but the norm remains: to be Black and become rich in America, you usually have to start by singing, dancing, making jokes, or running fast. This topic is examined in depth in author Michael Eric Dyson's (Princeton University) most recent book, *Entertaining Race: Performing Blackness in America*.

I hate this norm, but it's real. I wish the Black liberal arts creators involved with AfroTech got more shine. I wish serial entrepreneur Morgan DeBaun, who attended Washington University in St. Louis,

University of Hawai'i at Mānoa (PWI)
Honolulu, HI
13,000 Undergraduates
Public
Graduate Students: Yes
Setting: Urban

Temple University (PWI)
Philadelphia, PA
26,000 Undergraduates
Private
Graduate Students: Yes
Setting: Urban

was more visible and celebrated. As the founder and CEO of Blavity Inc., she is a media mogul who is not only making Black history; she's making Black present. And she has a liberal arts degree in political science and . . . wait for it . . . entrepreneurship! Ms. DeBaun is a wonderful exception and speaks to my declaration that, with a liberal arts degree, your child may be able to do anything. Similarly, there's Tristan Walker, founder and CEO of Walker and Company Brands, which includes Bevel Shaving and Form Beauty, who majored in economics at the State University of New York–Stony Brook. These are two stellar examples of Black people who are using their liberal arts degree to the maximum. I love them for this, for real, but I still believe that when we don't steer our children toward a wealth-building major in college, we are subjecting them to professional chance.

Washington University in St. Louis (PWI)
St. Louis, MO
7,600 Undergraduates
Private
Graduate Students: Yes
Setting: Urban

Stony Brook University, or the State University of New York at Stony Brook (PWI)
Stony Brook, NY
18,000 Undergraduates
Public
Graduate Students: Yes
Setting: Suburban

What Can You Do with a Liberal Arts Degree?

For anyone who's offended by what I've said, I want to be clear that there is not only one way to succeed. Success after graduation is determined by hustle and by your child identifying what they're good at and maximizing their potential. Many of my Black college friends have liberal arts degrees—most of them I went to Wesleyan with—and several of them are successful and happy. My point about leading your children toward specific majors is a product of the world being different now from what it was twenty to thirty years ago. While "jobs" are changing and may become obsolete in their traditional form, business and technology are booming, with companies like Apple, Google, and IBM no longer requiring college degrees for positions in their company. Many of us were in college during the tech boom of the mid-nineties and had little idea of the explosion that was about to happen. Imagine if AfroTech had not gotten such a late start? What if we could have closed the digital divide earlier? I want my children—and yours—to be on the cutting edge of innovation, and that may mean being a liberal arts major (rare) or a student who is attuned to where the world is moving.

While my feelings about this are strong, many of my education professional peers, Black and white, do not see it the same way. They are adamant that students should seek colleges that "match" or "fit" their unique profile and not be so set on one academic direction. One Black high school counselor we interviewed wished that more Black parents did not suggest engineering and business to their children. She implied that suggesting these majors and ensuing careers stifles children's creativity and does not allow them to create a career that may be better and maybe even more lucrative.

> "If there was one thing I would tell Black parents, [it's] that there are more than five majors. When talking with many families, the only majors they think exist are pre-med, engineering, law, business, and education. There are so many more majors and jobs than in those five areas. If I could get them to understand that, their college list would be a lot more realistic." (High school college counselor)

Her point is well taken. While some cultural groups historically have pushed their children toward certain majors, that's not what most Black people do, and I do not want to encourage a narrow view of acceptable majors. Part of how we have survived as a people is by being creative, innovative, and resourceful. Liberal arts education builds these capacities, and I would never want to be dismissive of it.

Here are some careers derived from liberal arts degrees according to *U.S. News and World Report*:

- Advertising representative
- Archivist
- Artist
- Events director
- Financial analyst
- Graphic designer

- Human resources specialist
- Journalist
- Marketing specialist
- Public relations specialist
- Project manager
- Research analyst
- Social worker
- Statistician
- Teacher
- Technical writer
- Web developer

So What Is a Parent's Role in This?

Black parents should assess who their children are and who they're becoming. We must educate ourselves and our children so that everyone understands the choices they have. A liberal arts education may be exactly what your child needs at this stage of their life. It may give them the chance to explore a range of academic disciplines they were not exposed to in high school and so tap into a curiosity that leads not just to a career but to genuine intellectual satisfaction and personal happiness. I applaud parents who love, accept, and support their children in this way and have more faith than fear. Some parents see a job and money as the necessary outcome of a college education. My advice is to partner with your child and have a joint vision for their educational and professional lives. We do not have to force them into anything, but we have to help them see how certain majors can lead to certain career opportunities. I think we should encourage them to take economics or finance or investing courses. To take a computer coding class maybe or to stick with a foreign language. What I do not like to hear is when parents say, "It's their life. They need to figure it out." No. This leads to students graduating college after more years than anticipated and oftentimes with more debt accumulated. While we know that each child is different and that some children will thrive in an environment where they can choose courses that stimulate their mind and lead them to become fascinating people, I urge you to make sure that there is a plan and a safety net. If your child does not know why they're in college, maybe they shouldn't be there, or they need an adult to steer them in a direction that builds on strengths they may not recognize. I am not saying that business, engineering, computer science, and pre-med are the only options, but I am saying to be wary of majors that do not have a direct correlation with employment and wealth-building.

I am aware that there are data to refute my assertions. Much of what I'm saying is anecdotal and may be emotionally tied to my being an educator and seeing too many of the Black students I have worked with graduate with a liberal arts degree and then feel "stuck" professionally. They do not regret their college experience; what they question is whether they made the right choice for their financial future when they selected a major.

In late 2021, I posed a question on my Facebook page: "For those who went to college or those who intend to send their children to college, do you find a liberal arts degree to be useful? Why or why not?" Responses were one-sided, and most people, regardless of race, defended their opinion that a liberal arts education is extremely valuable. The comment that challenged my thinking the most was this: "I think it's often unfairly painted as being impractical—I think it's actually highly practical and skills-oriented, especially in a largely information and knowledge-based economy." I think this was accurate and more than fair. Another person likened a liberal arts major to a "utility player" in baseball, which implies versatility. I could also call a liberal arts major a "jack of all trades and a master of none." Another comment was "It's part of an educational foundation, necessary to compete in many chosen professions. It's a path you can use to go to professional school." That last part supports a point of mine: earning a liberal arts education often requires that you go on to graduate school to level up. For many Black families, that move will bring more debt. Another comment that deserves to be quoted came from a friend: "The cost of college vs the debt ratio is alarming. The average number of students who complete within four years is less than 53%. The debt is debilitating for some. Most of the students I work with cannot afford to do it."

Money and college have a complicated relationship, and we will discuss it in chapter 12, "Show Me the Money."

I will always stand by the notion that cost, location, major, and career should be the core concerns when a family researches, applies to, and selects a college. I did not intend to convey the message that the liberal arts are bad or a one-way ticket to poverty. My hope is that this discussion of liberal arts as a luxury and pre-professional programs as a safer bet stirs your thinking about what's important for your family, the next educational steps for your child, and eventually both of your legacies. The next steps may not be immediately obvious, but now you have food for thought.

CHAPTER 6

What's Best for Your Child?

HBCUs versus PWIs

Overview

Throughout our children's educational experience we, as Black parents, must think about the spaces in which we place our children. College is no different. Currently, there is a divide among many Black families and college counselors about which is better: PWIs or HBCUs. While both have their own merits, there are a lot of misconceptions about which institution type will best prepare students for success. It is imperative that we parents help our children recognize their gifts and explore which kind of school may be best for their total development.

Some Black children need an HBCU for support, identity development, and personal comfort; others may thrive in any environment or may be more comfortable at a PWI because that is what they are accustomed to or because it has the type of diversity they seek. *HBCUs should at least be a consideration for your student given HBCUs' long track record of success across all disciplines.* However, if your vision for your child or, more importantly, their vision for themselves is of a PWI, make sure you have clear reasons for the choice and a plan for how to achieve success there.

At every stage of raising a child, we parents ask ourselves, "What will be best for my child?" In many of our life decisions, we do what we believe will give our children opportunities that we did not have or what we think would have benefited our own childhoods. We do our best to keep our children safe, healthy, and well educated. When it comes to their schooling, and according to our financial resources, we spend a lot of time considering their educational options: we evaluate the school district we reside in; we may weigh the pros and cons of private versus public education and estimate how much we are willing to pay for primary and secondary education; and we contemplate the many trade-offs we could make to help mold our children into who they will become. How will the school they attend affect their identity, development, and friend group? Will I as a parent have to worry about racism or other forms of discrimination? In a 2019 story in the *Washington Post* titled "The Tough Choices Black Parents Face When Choosing a School for Their Children," many parents interviewed for the story described the tough decisions they faced when examining educational choices. One parent called it the "head versus heart" dilemma. When a school that's a better option academically lacks racial diversity, there is almost always a price a Black child will pay in terms of their sense of self. As a parent, your head tells you that putting them in a high-ranking public school or private school is a smart decision. But your heart aches at the thought of what your child may have to endure there. There are so many factors that we as Black parents must consider to ensure that our children have the best chance at success and an equal opportunity. Just like many of our thoughts and actions as parents are informed by our personal experiences growing up, both good and bad, so are our perceptions of college.

When I (Tim) think back to the many things that drew me to my college of choice, I would say there was really no choice to be made. The choice was cemented in the brotherhood of Morehouse College, in the thriving Black affluence of the city of Atlanta, and with the deep indoctrination in Black culture that came with attending an HBCU. When I think back on those years at Morehouse, yes, my academic experience was rich and helped shape the person I became, but it was the environment, support, and the constant affirmation of who I was as a Black man that framed those years the most. I came from a predominantly white high school and community in

Arlington, Texas, and I found at Morehouse more than a college education; Morehouse helped me better understand my identity as a young Black man in America. The school gave me the confidence to go out into the world and instilled in me the necessity to serve. I understood my value and would not be discouraged by the many challenges of being Black in America.

My wife had a much different upbringing in Country Club Hills, a south suburb of Chicago. Her older brother attended Morehouse College, and her older sister went to Rust College. Her father completed his bachelor's and then a doctorate later in life at the University of Illinois at Chicago. No one outside her immediate family, however, had pursued higher education. As the youngest in the family who got some guidance from her siblings, she maintains that she was very misinformed about the process of the college search. She excelled in Advanced Placement courses, was involved in activities, and scored well on the ACT; however, with poor guidance, she applied to only two schools: Hampton University and the University of Miami. She chose to swap the harsh winters of Chicago for mild winters on the beaches of South Florida.

Rust College (HBCU)
Holly Springs, MS
623 Undergraduates
Private
Graduate Students: No
Setting: Remote

University of Illinois, Chicago (PWI)
Chicago, IL
22,000 Undergraduates
Public
Graduate Students: Yes
Setting: Urban

University of Miami (PWI)
Coral Gables, FL
11,000 Undergraduates
Private
Graduate Students: Yes
Setting: Urban

As she and I got to know each other as friends, one thing became evident: our college days were stark contrasts. Whereas I would talk about being on the yard and hanging out in Atlanta, she would tell me about watching games in the Miami Orange Bowl in the rain with more than sixty thousand fans, hanging out on South Beach, and wearing flip-flops all year long. And while my experience was defined by "traditional" Black culture and experiences, she was experiencing her Blackness in an entirely different way. Having graduated from a largely Black and Latinx high school, she found her transition to the University of Miami to be a bit of a shock. The campus exposed her to how variant being Black could be. She had her first experience being identified as an American Black among Bahamians, Jamaicans, and Haitians, together with affluent white, Cuban, and international classmates. My college experience largely strengthened my identity, yet she learned how to cling to hers differently. Naïvely drawn to the school because of the academics, beautiful campus, and strong sports reputation of "The U," she received a quick lesson in socioeconomics and experienced being an "only" in the classroom. While her time at Miami was rich in culture, there were moments defined by self-segregation, as described in the modern classic *Why Are All the Black Kids Sitting Together in the Cafeteria?* by Dr. Beverly Daniel Tatum, who is a Wesleyan University graduate and former Spelman College president.

During our time dating and in the early years of our marriage, we enjoyed talking about our different college experiences, along with the pros and cons that came with attending a PWI versus an HBCU. Our conversations were never about which one was better; rather, we talked about the experiences, socialization, and preparation for life that each type provided. We both considered ourselves successful in our professions, and neither of us questioned whether anything would have been better for us had we attended another college. It was not until we had children that the question arose. My wife dressed the children in Hurricanes clothes for Saturday games, while giving my mom the side-eye for putting them in University of Michigan gear, where she had attended as an undergraduate student in the 1960s. At the same time, I would talk about the day my son would attend Morehouse. Once they were toddlers, we had to think about where they may want to go to college and to imagine how those conversations would go. Like most parents who want their children to go to college, we would like our children to make informed decisions and do what is best for themselves.

University of Michigan (PWI)
Ann Arbor, MI
31,000 Undergraduates
Public
Graduate Students: Yes
Setting: Midsize City

In the introduction we said there are three camps of Black families on the question of HBCUs versus PWIs:

1. Those that believe PWIs are inherently better than HBCUs because they will offer their child a better chance at monetary success in life; these families will not consider HBCUs.
2. Those with parents who attended an HBCU and want their child to follow in their footsteps; these parents dismiss the idea of their child attending a PWI.
3. Those that will consider *all* institutions and let the decision be guided by financial aid or scholarships received, location, majors offered, and ultimately what's best for their family situation.

While the third camp is probably the largest, the first two make the most noise. Their preference usually drives the college search process. All three camps are justified in their thinking based on their lived experience; we do think it's very important, though, to enter the college search process with a mind open to both institutional types and to be guided by the needs of your child.

One of the best ways to identify which type is a better fit is simply to expose your child to both types of institution. Later in the book we will talk in depth about the college visit. To get a sense of what a school can offer, you can do no better than to walk around the campus, look at the buildings, talk to students and staff, and learn about the history of the school. Families living in the South and Mid-Atlantic have plenty of HBCUs within driving distance to visit. Families living in other parts of the country—the Midwest and the Mountain and Pacific time zones—live far from most HBCUs, the one farthest west being Langston University in Oklahoma. But

Langston University (HBCU)
Langston, OK
1,900 Undergraduates
Public
Graduate Students: No
Setting: Remote

Vanderbilt University (PWI)
Nashville, TN
13,000 Undergraduates
Private
Graduate Students: Yes
Setting: Urban

with proper planning, you can visit multiple campuses on a trip. For example, if you go to Nashville to visit Vanderbilt, be sure to visit Fisk and Tennessee State; if you go to Washington, DC, to see Howard, make stops also at American University, George Washington University, the University of Maryland, or Georgetown; you could then travel the short way to Baltimore to visit Johns Hopkins, Bowie State, and Morgan State; if you are in Atlanta looking at Georgia Tech or Emory, you could also look at Clark Atlanta, Morehouse, or Spelman; and if you go to New Orleans to tour Tulane, you can and should also visit Xavier and Dillard. In most major cities in the Central or Eastern time zone, you can tour both types of institution.

As you begin to think about the college search process, you must begin to evaluate as a family what is best for the student, with careful consideration of cost, location, major, and career. Moreover, given the current climate in the United States, we also encourage families to factor in how a school defines diversity, the resources and support it gives to Black students, and the cultural climate on its campus. We find that many parents and college counselors put a lot of emphasis on cost, location, major, and career and pay less attention to the social experiences outside formal education. Given all these factors, we think that Black families should consider both HBCUs and PWIs as viable options in their college search.

American University (PWI)
Washington, DC
8,000 Undergraduates
Private
Graduate Students: Yes
Setting: Urban

George Washington University (PWI)
Washington, DC
12,000 Undergraduates
Private
Graduate Students: Yes
Setting: Urban

University of Maryland (PWI)
College Park, MD
30,000 Undergraduates
Public
Graduate Students: Yes
Setting: Suburban

Georgetown University (PWI)
Washington, DC
5,500 Undergraduates
Private
Graduate Students: Yes
Setting: Urban

Bowie State University (HBCU)
Bowie, MD
5,400 Undergraduates
Public
Graduate Students: Yes
Setting: Suburban

Georgia Institute of Technology (PWI)
Atlanta, GA
16,500 Undergraduates
Public
Graduate Students: Yes
Setting: Urban

Emory University (PWI)
Atlanta, GA
7,000 Undergraduates
Private
Graduate Students: Yes
Setting: Suburban

Clark Atlanta University (HBCU)
Atlanta, GA
3,100 Undergraduates
Private
Graduate Students: Yes
Setting: Urban

Tulane University (PWI)
New Orleans, LA
7,700 Undergraduates
Private
Graduate Students: Yes
Setting: Urban

Dillard University (HBCU)
New Orleans, LA
1,100 Undergraduates
Private
Graduate Students: Yes
Setting: Urban

Understanding your child's level of self-awareness about their Black cultural identity should partially inform where you suggest they attend college. College should be a place where they will make progress as a young Black adult among other ambitious young Black adults. Historically, this has occurred at HBCUs and at prestigious PWIs such as Duke, the University of Virginia, Stanford, Northwestern, Georgetown, Emory, Wesleyan, and Amherst College. These schools have excellent reputations for having substantial, supportive Black populations with which students can engage during the college years and network after graduation. While none of the PWIs have the same level of intense HBCU familial love, if your child is a strong student, these schools need to be part of your exploration, according to your child's strengths and interests. There are many notable colleges and universities with great academic programs, facilities, and reputations of excellence, but we parents must ask ourselves a question: Do the schools have what my child needs to succeed both inside and outside the classroom?

In addition to cultural identity and the fit of a college campus, it's paramount that your student considers places where they feel they will be academically productive, be socially engaged, and have access to the tools they need to make moves toward a career. Throughout the college search process they must assess their strengths, weaknesses, and interests and determine what major or areas of study make the most sense for them in the short and long terms. There are any number of things that can help students fit in at a school such as connections with faculty, student organizations they identify with, support staff that help them navigate college life, and a campus that makes them feel they truly belong. The reality is that their interests will probably evolve, just as we parents continue to learn more about ourselves, but what is important is that they find schools that will give them options and won't limit their development in any way. College should not only be a place where students gain a formal education; it's also just as important, we would argue, that the college experience prepare them for self-leadership in their adult lives. Acclaimed author Malcolm Gladwell, in an interview on the College Guidance Network, advised students in the search for colleges to ask themselves the following questions:

1. What do I want my college experience to be like?
2. What do I care about?
3. What motivates me?
4. What do I stand for?

These are questions that need serious reflection early on as you begin the college admissions process.

Now, when we talk about HBCUs and PWIs, we must deal with the elephant in the room: *resources*. If there is one universal frustration expressed by parents and students about HBCUs compared with many elite PWIs, it's the physical plant. HBCUs' campus facilities (dorms, labs, gyms, etc.) and on-campus dining options are

Duke University (PWI)
Durham, NC
6,500 Undergraduates
Private
Graduate Students: Yes
Setting: Suburban

University of Virginia (PWI)
Charlottesville, VA
18,066 Undergraduates
Public
Graduate Students: Yes
Setting: Midsize City

Stanford University (PWI)
Palo Alto, CA
6,500 Undergraduates
Private
Graduate Students: Yes
Setting: Suburban

Northwestern University (PWI)
Evanston, IL
8,400 Undergraduates
Private
Graduate Students: Yes
Setting: Urban

Amherst College (PWI)
Amherst, MA
1,800 Undergraduates
Private
Graduate Students: No
Setting: Remote

sometimes not to families' liking. Couple that with the surrounding area of some HBCUs—southwest Atlanta, for instance, or Washington, DC. Some Black families fear their child is not "built" to navigate an environment with an element of the "hood." There have been several instances in helping and working with families that they have admitted that their child is unprepared for an HBCU environment without pristine landscaping or with an understandably jealous local population that likes to prey on young and naïve students. A similar worry, however, may keep these same students from enrolling on a rural PWI campus when they have lived their lives in suburban or urban neighborhoods and want to avoid being subjected to blatant racism.

In the interviews and roundtables we had with families, HBCU and PWI graduates, and college counselors, we asked why some Black families were resistant to considering HBCUs. In reply, all the groups had the perception that HBCUs are physically not as well equipped as their PWI counterparts. Some institutions like Harvard, Princeton, Yale, and Stanford have very large endowments that no HBCU could compete with, but resources extend beyond endowments. It's important also to think about what resources your individual student needs. Is it access to faculty and staff for academic support? Is it residential halls with programming for their academic interest? Intramural sports? Study abroad? Scholarships and financial aid? No matter what institutional type, a school may have all the resources most students want yet lack a certain resource your student discovers they desire. If you don't establish as a family what resources you need, you are doing a disservice to your student as you go through the college search process.

Too often, conversations about college are guided by rankings, reputation, legacy, and ego. While all of these reasons for considering a college hold value, are they in the best interest of the student and family? Higher education is a huge investment to make, so choosing a school should be given the same care as purchasing a home. Yes, everyone loves a beautiful home, but beyond its physical makeup, what matters most is its cost and the love it shelters.

When doing our research for this book, we heard about or from many families who had no real direction when they started the college admissions process. In most instances, this aimlessness came from having no certain answer to the essential question of "Why go to college?" Many will give an answer based on something external or in need of defining like satisfaction, pride, a good job, a nice salary, or the mythical idea that a college of university degree will open secret doors to success. By themselves, these reasons generally lack substance until somebody has spelled out what that substance is. Your *why* should be determined by your family's resources and the particular needs of the student. All we are asking is that you have the big-picture conversations about motives, means, and desired outcomes at the *beginning* of the admissions process and not near the end, at which time few decisions will remain that have not already been made for you.

The title of this chapter may be a bit misleading. We are not making an argument for either HBCUs or PWIs. There is no one clear answer for what type of school is better for all Black children. But we do implore Black families to have a firm understanding of the choices. We hope that you will repeatedly evaluate cost (debt), location, major, and career, while also giving priority to identity and campus amenities. Over all of these considerations is the umbrella of cultural experience that, as proud Black people, we cannot ignore, and we must help our children be proud of who they are in an environment that accepts them.

Above all, safety must be a priority: physical and emotional. There is no guarantee that any one environment will be better than another, but you must take your child's temperature about where they will be most comfortable and confident that they can succeed. Yes, there is the consideration that true growth happens in discomfort, but there is a time and a place for that. For students who are seventeen or eighteen years old, there are advantages to not placing them in a drastically unfamiliar environment to prove a point about their needing to be among Black people at an HBCU or needing to be forced into the "real world" of a PWI. Safety first.

PART II
X Factors

CHAPTER 7

What Questions Should You Be Asking in Your Family?

Overview

As your family begins to think about the educational choices facing your student, it's important to consider how those decisions will affect the college admissions process years down the line. Long before a student applies to college or even attends high school, many questions need to be considered:

1. How will you pay for your student's education?
2. Will your student attend public or private schools?
3. What courses will they need to take in preparation for college?

More than anything, your family needs to have clear and active communication early and often. You must know what questions each person involved should be asking as you plan for all aspects of the college admissions process—from academic, financial, and cultural perspectives.

―――――

Managing the partnership between parent and child during the admissions process is incredibly challenging. Like all partnerships, whether it be in a business, the game of spades, or a marriage, ideally it is a fifty-fifty relationship. We all know, however, that an even split is far from the reality in most instances. No matter what the nature of the relationship, communication is critical to reducing tension and misunderstanding. Communication will be paramount as your family begins the college admissions process and ultimately decides on a school that is beneficial for both child and family.

When it comes to parenthood, partnership takes on many forms. We would like to think that no matter the condition of the parents' relationship, their child's health and well-being, and a wish for the child's success in life, is something the parents can agree on. We believe that the ideal is to have two caring and responsible parents in a household, but we also know that this isn't everyone's reality or wish. Regardless of the makeup of the household, the educational choices made for a child from infancy through college can be difficult to make and, in many instances, require constant input from parents and caregivers. In a survey of Black parents, when asked if they agreed with their partner on educational philosophies, only 50 percent said yes and 28 percent said "for the most part." No matter whether you are part of a happily married couple or a single parent managing child-rearing alone, the conversation around educational choices for children is a complicated one.

Every family situation is unique, and it would be unrealistic for us to think that we can answer all of the questions that families will have about the college search. Still, we think it's important to address some of the fundamental ones. In appendix B, "Frequently Asked Questions," we provide many questions and answers that you can discuss as a family as you conduct your college search. Below, we provide some context for the questions to facilitate what can sometimes be challenging conversations.

Public versus Private

In our survey of Black parents, we found that, in many instances, their own K–12 educational experiences had a great deal of influence on how they wanted their children educated. In most cases, if both parents went to public school, they believed that public school would be adequate for their children, and those who went to private or independent school felt strongly that their children should have a similar educational experience. This holds true for Shereem and me (Tim) too. Shereem went to private school and has sent his children to private school as well. I went to public school and am a strong advocate of public school. What happens, however, when parents had different educational experiences? Now, we understand that for a lot of families, not just Black families, sending a child to an independent, boarding, or private school is not a viable option given the cost. We also understand that, depending on where you live, there may be few good public options, which further complicates this conversation and relates to a bigger conversation about equity of access to education. For those of us, however, who do have viable public and private options, the question of whether public or private school is the better option is a valid one to ask. There are pros and cons to both that you should take into consideration.

Here are some questions to think about:

1. Why is your family considering private school?
2. Does your student have particular needs?
3. Are there few good public options in your area?
4. Is there a particular curriculum offered by a private school that you think your child can benefit from?
5. Do you believe that private school can offer the best overall educational preparation for your child?
6. Is your family prepared to invest in private school in the formative years in addition to paying the cost of post-secondary education?

If you are thinking that going to a private school will automatically give your student a leg up in getting into a top college, that is simply not true. We address this topic in more depth in chapter 8, "Perception versus Reality."

The debate over private and public school often comes down to cost. In choosing to have your child attend public school, you may not be paying the school directly, but there are indirect costs if you are paying for a home or renting in a public school district in an affluent area. Thus, if you are considering public schooling for your child, the question of where you plan to live must be at the center of family conversations early on. Bear in mind that, compared with private schools, many public schools have larger class sizes, fewer individualized resources for students, and a more standardized curriculum, which can be limiting to some students. While most public schools do not have the small class sizes and rich resources of private schools, they often are more racially and socioeconomically diverse. If diversity is something that you and your family value, then that is a factor you'll want to weigh when considering educational options.

Is College the Best Option?

When many of us parents were growing up, we had three options after high school: go to college, join the military, or get a job. With the advent of the internet, social media, and online selling platforms like eBay and Etsy, there are new avenues open to making money and creating a business that were not available ten or fifteen years ago. Plus, many companies, such as Google and Apple, no longer require that applicants have a college degree to get hired. Given these new opportunities, many of them in entrepreneurship, parents may ask why their child has to go to college at all. While the data still point to postsecondary education creating higher levels of lifelong earnings, it's clear that there has been a significant shift in the labor marketplace and the preparation needed for entry. So, families should discuss whether college is the right plan for your student. Clearly things can change, but leading up to and through high school, everyone should be on the same page about whether going to college is a priority. The educational decisions made in preparation for college—in course selection, savings options, and extracurricular activities—are far different from decisions made when college is not the goal. In either case, everyone must agree on the plan before a student proceeds through high school because once the student enters high school, it can be hard to change their trajectory.

Our advice would always be to prepare in middle school and high school as though your child will go to college because, if there is a change in plan, it is much easier to shift when your student has a strong academic foundation than when they don't. It is during the formative years that students often develop their interests and passions. We believe that families should support these interests, but we don't think that support should come at the expense of the student's academic preparation, which can also help to nurture those interests. Regardless of the student's trajectory, it's important to discuss what the long-term goals are. Some students are just not meant to go to college, and that's fine. There are students who are destined to be soldiers, and there are those whose entrepreneurial spirit will drive their life choices. There is no right or wrong way to go, but it's important that parents and guardians have a plan in place.

Funding College

If there is agreement that the goal is college, then the conversation about how the student's college education will be paid for must happen early on. College is expensive, and the cost of college is not going down anytime soon.

I (Tim) have often said getting into college is easy; paying for college is the hard part. Yes, there are a lot of schools that offer great financial aid to support families, but the truth is that the more money and assets you have as a family, the less need-based aid you are likely to be offered by financial aid offices. Given how aid is calculated, many middle- and upper-class families have difficulty securing the financial aid they believe they deserve. This can be frustrating to families who fall into this category; thus the parents in these families should talk to their child about how they are going to pay for and save for college sooner rather than later. These conversations may influence the decision of where the child can apply.

Additionally, with the evolution of affirmative action and how it's regulated, the idea of a "minority" scholarship is not as pervasive as it was thirty years ago. So, if you are counting on scholarship money to help fund your child's college experience, that is a possibility you'll want to explore prior to their senior year. In chapter 12, "Show Me the Money," we discuss financial aid in some detail.

How Far Away Is Too Far?

Families must ask early on, "How far away is too far? Are there any geographical limits to the schools your student will apply to?" With social media, email, and teleconferencing technology made popular in the pandemic, it's easy to stay connected at a distance, but there are other factors to consider related to a school's location. Public colleges and universities located outside your family's state of residence will charge higher tuition to out-of-state students. There is also the expense of plane or train tickets if students decide to go to a school far from home. Finally, there is the consideration for parents of how long it will take to reach their child should something happen. Families may be open to negotiating the matter of distance, but the matter should be addressed early in the college search process to manage expectations for everyone.

Over 50 percent of all college students attend schools less than a hundred miles from home. Only 16 percent of students travel five hundred miles or more from home to attend college.

In addition to distance, there is also the question of *where* parents are willing to let their children go to school. When we spoke with parents in preparing to write this book, several parents were adamant about states and regions where they would not want their students to attend school. One family said, "We know our daughter is looking to play Division I volleyball in college, but there are certain schools that we know we are not even going to consider because we worry about our daughter being in certain states." While much of this hesitancy and concern is driven by the current social climate in the country, it is also driven by regional bias, stereotypes, and personal experiences. One parent explained, "I know I would not want my student to apply to [school X] because when I visited there when I was applying to college in the eighties, I was called the

N-word and would not want my child considering it even if it is now considered one of the top schools in the country."

Although this event happened nearly forty years ago, such events can stick in a parent's memory and influence where they feel comfortable sending their children to school. Many would argue that a lot has changed in our country since the eighties and nineties, but the counterargument can be made that little has changed. If there are locations that parents have concerns with, it is important that they explain to their child where the concerns come from. Finally, we would encourage parents to reach out to schools they have concerns with and ask those schools how they are supporting Black students and ensuring their academic success, safety, and cultural support.

Return on Investment

We started this chapter talking about partnerships. For any partnership you have, you want it to be a success, and how success is defined varies. Everyone is looking for return on investment, or ROI, and the college experience is no different. When families begin to think about college, they must determine what college success looks like.

1. Is success graduating and being debt free?
2. Is it finishing in four years with a job in hand?
3. Is it being able to say you attended one of the top institutions in the country?
4. Is there some other standard that will define success for your student in the college experience?

The reality is that apart from attending a school for brand recognition, the other criteria of success can be met at many institutions in the country.

It is easier, of course, to access certain resources and opportunities at some institutions than at others. If a student decides to attend Emory and is interested in pre-med, do they have an advantage over a student at Agnes Scott College or Georgia State University when it comes to access to hospitals and clinics? Maybe, due

Agnes Scott College (PWI)
Decatur, GA
1,000 Undergraduates
Private
Graduate Students: No
Setting: Suburban

Georgia State University (PWI)
Atlanta, GA
22,000 Undergraduates
Private
Graduate Students: Yes
Setting: Urban

to proximity. But does having access to those resources guarantee a greater chance of admission to medical school than students have at the other schools? **No.** We hope that you will take away many messages from this book, but one of them is that name and or brand recognition will only go so far. Many people think that if their child goes to school X, then things will be easier upon graduation, but the reality is that schools at all levels are looking for the best students, not average students who happened to attend good schools. Only you and your family can define what success is in the college experience. If there is an experience your family is looking for from college, begin discussing it early.

What's Driving the Decision-Making?

In *The Truth about College Admission*, authors Brennan Barnard and Rick Clark describe four critical areas, or wedges as they call them, that often trip families up as they navigate the college search process: time, communication, money, and ego. We have addressed the importance of starting early, having clear communication, and discussing money, and we also want to discuss what may be the biggest obstacle in the process: the presence of ego. Barnard and Clark are forthright about how families should approach the admissions experience: "For the sake of family relationships, parents and students must put their egos in the box." When it comes to the ego of Black parents, we know that some parents are determined that the money they spend on their child's higher education is going to the HBCU from which they graduated, whereas others think that HBCUs are inferior schools and so don't consider them at all for their child. What should be driving the process of selecting a school, however, is what is best for the student's development.

Should parents have a say in the college search process? Of course. We advocate for that throughout the book, but it is the student, after all, who will have to live with the decision that gets made. We would hope that there is room for the student to articulate what they are looking for and to explore the many college options available to them. It's important that the student have a voice that is listened to and respected. In other words, everyone involved needs to keep an open mind.

Families, as you embark on the college admissions process, count on coming across challenges along the way. Some of these will be relatively simple to sort out, such as deciding how many schools is enough to apply to, while others will be more difficult, such as helping a student cope with rejection letters. The admissions process has changed so much over the past twenty-five years and continues to do so.

There is a joke in college admissions that the answer to any question is "it depends." How much financial aid will I receive? It depends. What are my chances of getting in? It depends. Can I graduate in four years? It depends. Will I have a job or acceptance to a graduate school upon graduation? It depends. The college search process can be confusing and complicated without proper direction. That is why there is a booming industry of independent college counseling professionals—like Shereem's company Strategic Admissions Advice—that help families navigate the college search process. Many of these admissions consultants are great at what they do because of their understanding of the process and access to information, but their greatest strength is in providing direction to families, and that begins with knowing what colleges are looking for and what questions to ask a family to find the right fit. Similarly, in this chapter we gave you context for the fundamental questions you should be asking in your family to bring clarity when the college search begins, clarity that comes from understanding the *why* behind your search.

CHAPTER 8

Perception versus Reality

Overview

College admissions is a mysterious process, and each school has its own set of standards for decision-making. As families begin the college search process, there are a lot of assumptions they may make from not understanding the context and nuances of admissions or from having wrong information picked up from the "wine and cheese circuit," as we like to call it. We have spent a lot of time answering families' questions about the mysteries of college admissions, and we have certainly spent time dispelling myths and correcting misinformation that spreads through neighborhoods and schools. In this chapter we explore some of the most common misperceptions that add to the anxiety already built into college admissions.

There are a lot of things that stand out in our almost fifty years of combined work in secondary and higher education. One of these is the disconnect between perception and reality surrounding the college admissions process. Oftentimes people have strong opinions about what it takes to get into top schools or what goes into preparing a strong application. Many of these opinions are held by parents who saw their child get into their first-choice school. Sometimes an admissions officer claims to have an insider track and offers advice that is not applicable to every institution. **In reality, there is no formula that guarantees admission at top colleges and universities**. Most admissions decisions are influenced by an individual school's needs, or what we in the profession call "institutional priorities." These priorities can vary from year to year and may take into account athletic programs, development (institutional advancement or donations), geography, academic interest, the need for members in the marching band or on the debate team, the desire for a student from a specific state, or any number of other priorities that institutions consider in composing their incoming class.

PWIs Are Better Than HBCUs

One of the most surprising things we found from one of our surveys of Black parents was that 92 percent of them believe that there is a perception that PWIs are "better" than HBCUs.

"As I was going through my college admission process, it was made clear to me by my college counseling office that in order for me to be successful, I should attend a PWI. Morehouse was viewed as a safety school." (Graduate of the University of Virginia)

"Our daughter knew she wanted to go to a competitive school like University of Pennsylvania or another of the Ivies; she ultimately ended up at Columbia through Early Decision. But as she was going through the process, Spelman was never an option, despite my efforts, and a lot of that had to do with the culture of her independent school. The fact that not many students considered HBCUs mainly because there is a lack of HBCU exposure in California." (Alumni of Spelman and Williams College)

University of Pennsylvania (PWI)
Philadelphia, PA
10,000 Undergraduates
Private
Graduate Students: Yes
Setting: Urban

Williams College (PWI)
Williamstown, MA
2,000 Undergraduates
Private
Graduate Students: No
Setting: Remote

We understand the many reasons for this survey finding, yet there is a fundamental question here about what makes up "better." Is better having more resources? A larger endowment? Is better being diverse? Or is better simply a matter of name recognition or ranking by *U.S. News and World Report?* Many don't know that those rankings are calculated with variables that are not directly related to students' undergraduate experience on campus. Some of the variables include the school's selectivity based on test scores and class rank, the rate of alumni giving, and the academic reputation of the school, but ethnic and racial diversity are currently not calculated in the rankings. There may be solid arguments for why the ranking variables are what they are, but it can also be argued that they do not speak directly to student experiences, the support services offered, or the campus climate that students will experience daily. Thus, if you emphasize rank when selecting schools, it's important that you understand what those rankings mean for your child.

To answer the question of whether HBCUs or PWIs are better, you must define what *better* means to you. So often, *better* is defined by someone outside your home or by circumstances or variables that don't speak directly to your child's needs. There can be so many things that go into determining whether something is better, and the reality is that it's subjective. Most college graduates, no matter what type of school they went to, think their school is better than others for any number of reasons. As we enter the college search process with our children, however, we can't depend solely on what we think we know. It's important that we keep an open mind, do the research, visit the campuses, and think beyond ourselves and our social circles.

Black Lives Matter

Yes, Black lives matter in college admissions, but the reality is that all lives matter in college admissions, especially given the 2023 ruling by the US Supreme Court that overturned the legality of using race as a criterion in college admissions. Affirmative action policies that had existed in the 1970s, 1980s, and 1990s are no longer legal, which will hinder colleges and universities from forming entering classes that meet their goals for racial diversity. For students looking to apply to elite PWIs such as Harvard University and the University of North Carolina at Chapel Hill, the two institutions named in the Supreme Court cases, the court's decision is a setback. With no actual data yet to gauge how this decision will play out in practice, we recommend that students find ways to present their identity and lived experience in the essays they write for applications. Now, more than ever, essays will be a crucial part of an application in the decision-making process.

One thing to know when you come across the word *diversity* in higher education is that its meaning is inclusive and comprehensive. When many of the parents who are reading this book went to college, schools recruited Black, Hispanic, and Native students directly; today, schools use much more inclusive terms like *underrepresented*, *students of color*, or *BIPOC*. These terms are more inclusive, yes, but they also lump groups together as though they were all the same. Thus, when having conversations about diversity on college campuses, it's important to be intentional in the language you use. If you ask about Black students, they may be grouped under these umbrella terms, which may not yield the answers you are looking for. In many

The Supreme Court on Affirmative Action before Its Decision in 2023

1978: In *Regents of the University of California v. Bakke,* the court ruled that the medical school at the University of California, Davis, could not reserve some slots with separate admissions standards for minority applicants. But the court also ruled that colleges could consider race and ethnicity in admissions decisions in ways that did not create quotas.

2003: In *Gratz v. Bollinger,* the court ruled that the University of Michigan at Ann Arbor had unconstitutionally used an undergraduate admissions system in which underrepresented minority applicants received points for their ethnicity or race.

2003: In *Grutter v. Bollinger,* the court ruled that the University of Michigan's law school was within its constitutional rights in considering applicants' race or ethnicity because it did so through a "holistic" review and not by simply awarding points for race or ethnicity.

2013: In *Fisher v. University of Texas at Austin,* the court ruled that lower courts needed to apply "strict scrutiny" and not give colleges deference when reviewing legal challenges to colleges' consideration of race and ethnicity in admissions decisions.

Source: https://www.insidehighered.com /news/2016/06/24/supreme-court -upholds-consideration-race-admissions

BIPOC stands for
Black, Indigenous,
People of Color

instances *diversity* refers to geographic origin, citizenship, socioeconomic status, being first generation, and other factors. *Diversity*, especially at PWIs, has become this catch-all term to keep in step with the growing diversity, equity, and inclusion initiatives in our country, but how schools define *diversity* may change based on the audience. Both PWIs and HBCUs are looking to expand the diversity on their campuses, given the changing demographics of our country and heightened awareness of a need for greater access and social justice.

Going to a "Good" High School Helps

Can going to a competitive high school help you in your college preparation? Yes. Does going to a high school (public or private) with a good reputation ensure you will get into the college of your choice? No. Not everyone has a good public school in their neighborhood to attend, with a curriculum and resources to support the multiple needs of its students. With any school that you send your student to, your student must take advantage of the opportunities and the resources available. So often I (Tim) review applications from students from private schools, where the students got good grades but did not take advantage of the academic and extracurricular opportunities offered at the schools given all their resources. When I see this, I am frustrated because many of these students have had plentiful opportunities, but they did not challenge themselves like their peers did. There is a belief in some Black families that if they just send their child to a "good" high school and the child does well, the name of the school will open doors to colleges and universities that would not have opened had they attended a school of less renown. Yes, there are instances when this happens, but colleges and universities focus on what the student did while at that school in comparison with their peers. Going to a competitive school can put a student in a hyper-competitive environment for which they may not be prepared. When it comes to top colleges and universities, where a student attended high school really means relatively little when stacked against what they were able to do with what they encountered there.

Shereem and I know parents who put too much stock in the caliber of the secondary school their child attended. We recently spoke to a mother whose son attended a well-regarded independent school. She was hopeful, bordering on confident, that he would be admitted to an Ivy League school given his high SAT score. He was *not* a straight-A student, but he had been involved in extracurricular activities that she expected to play in his favor on applications. This family later had a rude awakening when the son did not get into any of the Ivies and was waitlisted nearly everywhere else. Ultimately he had one college option open to him, and it was for a school where the family had never intended him to go.

The family had operated under the false assumption that the reputation of the son's high school, coupled with his leadership in activities and high test score, would trump his above-average, though not stellar, grades. Yes, he had taken some rigorous courses, but his grades were not consistently high; and in the application pool of selective schools, his leadership in activities was probably typical for applicants. If the student would have applied to 95 percent of the other colleges and universities in this country, he would have stood a better chance of being admitted. But having a limited scope for "success" had compelled the family to apply to a narrow set of schools, and the result was one offer of admission that did not satisfy their expectations.

We tell this story because too often we find that everyone thinks they're an expert when it comes to college admissions. Parents absolutely do know their child best and no doubt want what is best for them through the admissions process, but they may bring to the process assumptions they gathered from the rumor mill or heard from the "street committee." When false information conditions their perception, families can make uninformed decisions, and the child winds up being the one who suffers for it.

We always encourage parents and students to reach out to schools to ask them the questions they want answered. Families, it is imperative that you seek clarification on things that are not clear to you; above all, think about the student's mental health over institutional ranking or reputation. Months after the admissions process is over, there'll come a day when your new college student finds themselves alone on campus, perhaps sitting in their dorm room. They will have an adult moment of reflection and take in the reality of the college choice they have made. One admissions veteran reminded us of the wisdom in a famous Mike Tyson quote: "everyone has a plan until they get punched in the mouth." We want families to have ambitious, balanced, and carefully considered plans, which mark a path to success that isn't narrower than it needs to be. Be ready for the unseen punch: have plans B, C, and D in reserve, instead of simply hoping that plan A will work out.

Testing: Does It Matter?

In chapter 15, we will go into depth about standardized testing and how it fits into the admissions process, but here we provide a quick assessment of how testing is perceived. The truth is that it varies among colleges. COVID-19 made many more schools become *test-optional*, *test-blind*, or some other variation that gives students the option to submit scores. It will be interesting to see how institutions and testing agencies respond when things return to normal. Some schools may remain test-optional, joining the subset of schools that were test-optional prior to the pandemic. These schools can be found at FairTest, fairtest.org. However, many colleges and universities in the country will likely go back to requiring tests in some fashion, rejoining those that never suspended the requirement.

Students can have a great test score, but no matter how great it is, it probably will not take precedence over the courses and grades on a student's transcript through their high school career. The same is true on the other end of the spectrum. A student may have what is perceived to be a low test score; however, if they have taken rigorous courses and have good grades, that low test score might be overlooked. When you think about testing, it's best to remember that it's just a number; and for the most selective schools in the country, know that it takes more than just a single number, whether GPA or test score, to be admitted.

The Rumor Mill

We want to make sure that you are aware that all information is not good information. When it comes to college admissions, we have discovered that many people who have gone through the process one or two times feel equipped to share information about how the process works. What we like to call "admissions fake news" is something you will often hear on the "wine and cheese circuit." This happens when gossipy parents exaggerate stories when they don't know why their student was admitted. All parents want their children to be seen in the best light, and what they say happened in admissions is probably just a small part of the file that resulted in the applicant's admission. There are perceptions of what it takes to get into selective schools that are far from the reality. We want you to be informed about the realities that take place in admissions and not depend on misguided information given how subjective admissions can be.

As you and your family explore colleges, we encourage you to use all the resources at your disposal. While we are happy you are reading this book, this is just one of many resources. We advise you to research each school you are looking at and be in communication with its admissions staff, who will give you the right information to help separate perception from reality.

Case Study

We conclude this chapter with a thought exercise that we invite you to complete. High school and college admissions offices often use *case studies* to put students and parents in the seat of an admissions officer, from where they get a glimpse at how decisions are made based on class needs and institutional priorities. Imagine that you are an admissions officer for a university and must determine the **one** student out of four who will be admitted to the incoming class. Review the profiles of the four students in the table on the next page and read the institutional statistics and priorities listed below before making your determination.

All four applicants are applying to the university's College of Arts and Sciences. The university has asked its admissions officers to consider the following when reviewing applicants:

- The university is looking for outgoing students who will add to the university community.
- Average GPA of the students admitted last year: 3.4.
- The university is test-optional; however, 50 percent of last year's applicants opted to submit scores. The average scores of last year's admitted students were 1150 for the SAT and 24 for the ACT.

The university wants its admissions officers to make the following decisions about the four applicants:

- Admit (1)
- Waitlist (1)
- Deny (2)

Be assured that our case study is oversimplified. There are other factors used to evaluate applicants, of course—among them: essays, letters of recommendations, and the rigor of high school courses taken.

Case Study

Attribute	Student 1	Student 2	Student 3	Student 4
Gender	Male	Female	Female	Male
GPA	3.2	4.0	3.5	2.9
Test score	ACT 23	Did not submit	SAT 1000	ACT 33
High school	Independent	Public	Charter	Home-schooled
Activities	President of student government association, member of school band, involved in church	Worked 30 hours a week in high school, very little school involvement	Started robotics club, president of chemistry club, Girl Scout	Trained for an Olympic sport
Other information	Both parents are doctors	Single-parent household, parent did not attend college	Lives with mother, who went to college and is a corporate executive	Both parents have a college degree and have their own business

Decision:
admit (1)
waitlist (1)
deny (2)

CHAPTER 9

Why We All Need to Prioritize Mental Health

Overview

So far, we have tried to guide you in how to navigate the philosophical and logistical parts of the college admissions process. We feel it is essential at this juncture to shine a light on the mental health of students and parents when they go through the process. We understand the roller coaster of emotions and complex of expectations that come with applying to college. Collectively—students, parents, and educators—need to work together to manage anxiety and expectations throughout.

As families work through the college admissions process, they will spend a lot of time focusing on grades, test scores, and extracurricular activities. What they often overlook, though, is the emotional toll the process can take on students and parents alike. We, as parents and guardians, want to protect our children from any disappointment, while at the same time making sure they have everything they need to succeed. When it comes to choosing our child's primary and secondary schools, we can exercise some control, but when our child applies to college, especially to selective schools, we find there is next to nothing we can do to ensure our child's admission to a preferred institution.

In the book *Excellent Sheep: The Miseducation of the American Elite and the Way to a Meaningful Life*, William Deresiewicz, a former Yale professor, critiques how our nation's secondary and higher education systems, along with some parents, do not promote critical thinking in students. Instead, too often we maintain the status quo by following the same formula of cautioning students not to take risks in their course selections and pushing them toward pre-professional programs. Deresiewicz claims that one of the main reasons the admissions process can be so devastating is that high-achieving students and parents who are accustomed to getting what they want are suddenly forced to deal with hearing *no*.

Rejection is hard to accept, but in college admissions, it is often the final answer. We understand that not everyone is interested in elite colleges, but many of you reading this book are, so we need to tell you a hard truth. These "elite" schools have alarmingly low admit rates, lack genuine racial and cultural diversity, and, in many respects, cost the most. We urge you, parents and students with eyes fixed on elite schools, to reconsider what you prioritize and to redefine success in order to minimize the anxiety and stress that come with college admissions.

As we emphasize throughout the book, the college admissions process is individualized and varies from family to family. However, in our conversations with, and surveys of, parents, educators, and mental health professionals, we have learned of some best practices for supporting students and parents. College admissions will always and unavoidably bring some degree of confusion and angst, but our goal is to equip families with tools to keep their children healthy and hopeful through senior year of high school.

Dr. Bianca Busch, a board-certified psychiatrist who specializes in counseling college-age young people (www.collegepsychiatrist .com), has advice on matters we address in this chapter. One of her mantras is that we, as parents, must learn to compromise with our teens. Rarely will a student get everything they want, just as a parent will not get everything they want. The goal for a parent must be to partner with their student and have open communication, with an understanding that the student's social and emotional well-being is most important. This is not an easy ask, of either party, but it is imperative for maintaining a productive family relationship.

In making suggestions for best practices, we have divided the chapter into three sections for three different audiences: (1) parents, (2) students, and (3) schools, secondary and postsecondary. While all these groups should be working together, we explain how each can take responsibility for keeping mental health at the forefront of the discussion.

Parents

Parents, we hate to be the bearer of bad news, but you may be one of the biggest reasons for stress in the college admissions process. Throughout this book, **we encourage parents to manage their expectations while supporting the goals and aspirations of their child.** Too often these two things are not aligned. In a research study, Encoura, a company focusing on data science regarding students and higher education, found that parents and students generally agree that a desirable institution of higher education should be high-quality, affordable, and friendly. Where their views diverge, however, is on the value of "brand." Parents prefer an institution that is well known and prestigious to a greater degree than do students, who want an institution to be career-centered and fun. Often parents form their opinions about a school based on corporate experiences or on their own experiences from twenty or thirty years ago, whereas students think about what their near-term experience in college will be.

There are some merits to prioritizing schools with a recognizable name, but there is more to the college experience than an institution's notoriety. Thus, a frank family conversation about what makes a school desirable should take place early in the admissions process to flush out any divergent or conflicting values. We implore parents to keep an open mind and to understand that an education from an elite institution is not a golden ticket to success and happiness. A conversation may reveal that your student wants something qualitatively different from a school than what you want for them. (Ouch!

But that's okay.) We encourage parents to relax, knowing all too well that relaxing requires a lot of self-composure, and to allow the process to unfold. As long as you are working together as a family transparently, your child will land on their feet.

For families that want to pursue admission to the most selective schools in the country, we ask that you understand how competitive admission is and evaluate whether a highly selective school is the best fit for your student academically, socially, and emotionally. If your child experiences great disappointment when they don't make a high grade or rank highly in their class, attending a competitive school could be harmful to their self-esteem. No, we are not advocating that we crush our children's dreams, but we would advise parents to be up front about the low probability that any student who applies to a highly selective college will get in. If a school has a 15 percent rate of admission, help your student understand what 15 percent means, which is easier to do when you have available the average GPA and test scores of the school's admitted class from last year.

A major culprit of adding stress to the college admissions process is believing misinformation that could come from comparing your student's situation to anyone else's. A decision made years ago of where to attend college may rest on reasons that no longer apply. If you find yourself taking advice, especially unsolicited advice, from people outside the profession of college counseling, you may be setting a foundation for the college search on shifting sand. We caution you to be skeptical of others' advice, but please don't feel like you have to do this on your own! Instead, seek out assistance from professionals in college counseling. In the event that you don't agree with the advice from a school counselor, reach out to someone affiliated with the National Association of College Admission Counseling, or NACAC for short.

Talking about the college admissions process can be overwhelming to both students and parents; thus it's important not to make it a topic of conversation every day. A college admissions veteran of more than twenty years told us how he had made this very mistake. When it came time for his own son to go through the process, he brought the subject up daily, and that made it all only that much more stressful. His son told him as much. The two then decided they would talk about college applications only once a week. Once they set a weekly time to discuss timelines, schools, and related items, the process went a lot better. The teenage-self-development years are stressful enough without ever tossing college admissions into the mix, so, parents, please build some parameters for college talk in your home. Be mindful that your job as a parent is not only to support your student in the admissions process but also to validate and support their feelings as much as possible.

Finally, parents, you must talk about money as a family, early and often. We know of far too many instances where family discussion of affording college was never more than vague. If your child is aiming for a "dream school" and you have concerns about how you will afford it, you're setting yourself up for stress if you keep those concerns to yourself. We have seen students get admitted to their dream school, and only then do their parents have the tough conversation about what they can and cannot afford. Too often, where to apply for college is the only family financial decision that parents leave in their child's hands. In no other situation would we allow a teenager to make a decision that could cost anywhere from $30,000 to $300,000. Waiting until senior year to talk about paying for college is not fair to the student or to your family. There is no way to begin the college admissions process productively and transparently without talking about money and making it a guiding factor in the process.

In chapter 12, "Show Me the Money," we give an overview of financial aid, but long before you ever complete any financial aid forms, your family must have active communication about resources so that your child understands any limitations. This communication between child and parents about finances is an important developmental milestone and serves as a soft launch for the greater independence that comes with attending college.

We end our advice to parents with an apology for the waitlisting and deferring commonly done by colleges and universities, which we know is a frustrating extension to what has already been a long wait to hear a decision. One reason why institutions waitlist and defer applicants liberally is that they must compensate for students who have applied to multiple schools—sometimes to the tune of twenty-five to thirty at a time. Such a number is excessive, which is why we recommend that students apply to between seven and twelve schools. As long as schools must hedge their bet on how many admitted students will actually enroll, they have to keep applicants on hold, as reserves, until the number of enrolled students in an entering class has met their target.

Students

As you begin the process of college admissions, we want to give you a few important pieces of advice. First of all, **do not compare yourself to others**. Every college application is unique just like the student who submits it, so comparing yourself to another student implies that you and that other person are the same, and we know that not to be true. In my (Tim's) twenty-plus years working in college admissions, I have never put two applications side by side and made a decision by comparing them; rather, each decision that an admissions officer makes is based on the individual merits of that student in the context of the larger applicant pool.

Another piece of advice: **never wait until the last minute to begin any part of your applications**. Preparing ahead of time relieves stress and allows for your application and essays to be thought through. Most applications open for submission on August 1, with the earliest deadlines set as soon as October 15. The most common deadline is January 1. In addition, many essay prompts and application instructions become open to viewing during the summer before a student's senior year, meaning there is plenty of time for students to create a timeline of steps, draft their essays, and work with their college counselor to meet all deadlines. Since most students will apply to multiple colleges, they must not wait until deadlines are on top of them. A pending deadline can be a significant stressor when it forces you to rush through getting an application ready. Creating timelines and adhering to them, and having a strategic application plan, can relieve much of the inevitable pressure of senior year.

One last piece of advice: **remember that you are not alone in this process**. You have your family, college counselors, and a school community who is there to support you. If there is ever a moment you are feeling overwhelmed, anxious, or doubtful, reach out to someone in your community for some help. That might be a parent. Or you may find it easier to talk with someone in the college counseling office at your high school who better understands the process. Depending on what you are feeling, you may also want to seek out a guidance counselor or therapist. No matter what your worry is, there is nothing wrong with asking for support beyond the completion of applications. The goal of the college admission process should be completing high school and being excited about the next chapter of your life.

Schools, Secondary and Postsecondary

High schools promote college and congratulate themselves when they have a notable percentage of their graduates accepted to certain colleges and universities. Oftentimes, these esteemed institutions are selective ones. This attention paid to a subset of schools can give students the wrong impression that educational success depends on their attending one of them.

To support our students and their mental health, we must assure them that success does not derive from the name of the school they attend but rather from what they do with their time and opportunity there. In this book we try to enlarge and illuminate success by profiling the alma maters of amazing Black college graduates like billionaires Oprah Winfrey (Tennessee State University) and David

Steward (Central Missouri State University), neither of whom attended a school you'll find celebrated in *U.S. News and World Report.* This message of expanding success must be amplified for our students. We have to share with them that there are more than four thousand colleges and universities around the country and not just the one hundred we see listed in *U.S. News and World Report* or whose sports teams we watch play on ESPN. By paying attention beyond this narrow group of high-profile, ranked schools, we can help lessen students' anxiety around higher education as it relates to success.

We want you, school counselors, administrators, and teachers to expand the list of schools you are recommending. Truth be told, many of you make lists limited to your lived experience or generated by Scoir, Naviance, MaiaLearning, or some other platform for CRM (customer relationship management) in college admissions. These lists for Black families are often uninspired. To those who work in high schools, we ask that you educate yourselves about the cultural needs/desires of a student's family and, even more so, educate yourself on schools that have proven themselves to be supportive of Black students.

As for college admissions offices, we hope you will speak plainly and transparently with all families when you share information. College admissions officers may use terms like *admit rate, yield, holistic review, test-optional, rigor,* and others without providing enough context to help families appreciate the real probability of their student being admitted.

In response to our survey on mental health that we sent out to admissions professionals, one of the best suggestions we got for preserving emotional well-being through the admissions process was for institutions to be more "responsible" in their use of deferrals and waiting lists. Students and families have already waited for weeks or months to hear a decision to their application, so making these families wait even longer for a response when there is no time table for one only adds to their stress. While I (Tim) understand the need for deferring and waitlisting from an enrollment management standpoint, the number of students placed in these holding patterns is excessive, and usually very few of them are eventually admitted. We understand that no one wants to hear **no**, but stringing along students and their families for weeks or months later than necessary is even worse. Better it is to "rip off the Band-Aid" and let those rejected move on in their plans.

Limiting the stress and anxiety caused by the college admissions process is the shared responsibility of all involved. Everyone needs to be more **intentional**. Students and their parents must be more intentional about the schools they apply to, considering cost, location, academic major, and career. College admissions officers should be more intentional about which applicants they defer and place on the waiting list by evaluating whether those applicants have a realistic chance of getting in. Holding an application hostage when the student's likelihood of acceptance is remote can be mentally exhausting and unfairly so.

There is already enough anxiety and stress built into this process without us adding to it. We must collectively make mental health a priority, and each of the aforementioned constituencies plays a role in that. Students must take responsibility for their well-being and ask for help and direction as they work on applying to college. Parents and school counselors must work together to identify schools that will not only support a student's academic growth but also their social and emotional development. We are here to help young people grow, make mistakes, learn, and ultimately excel. These are tender years, those from eighteen to twenty-two, and we need to give students the tools they'll require to succeed in adulthood. Secondary and postsecondary schools must be committed to providing students with appropriate guidance and information. Remind students, too, that success is not simply determined by grades or test scores or class rank or by the college or university they ultimately attend. Success is personal and has no one path leading to it.

Finally, we all need to factor in how we use social media. Yes, social media is an excellent way to share information and highlight the accomplishments of students and schools. However, it also can serve as the primary barometer of what success looks like, which is what happens when only some students and schools are highlighted. What message does it send to future college students and their families when only selective schools are praised? Let us be clear, we are not saying that everyone deserves a trophy or not to celebrate individuals' accomplishments, but we do strongly request that we all be mindful of the power of social media in how it can shape narratives for this generation.

While it may sound cliché to say it, the goal in life should be happiness. Happiness does not come from students being admitted to a certain school or from their academic achievements but rather from being thoughtful about the decisions they make. We all must help students make good decisions, not ones calculated to win outward validation from grades or other metrics but ones that will bring them well-being and purpose as they begin their adult lives. Happiness is a choice, and we must make it a focus in the college admissions process.

CHAPTER 10

Gender Wars

How Black Males and Black Females
Are Assessed in College Admissions

Overview

When we wrote the first edition of our book, affirmative action was practiced by most colleges and universities. After the Supreme Court's ruling in June 2023, that will no longer be the case. We do still think it necessary to discuss the influence of gender on how students are evaluated in college admissions.

There is a growing gender imbalance throughout US higher education at both PWIs and HBCUs. Among Black students applying to college, this imbalance is amplified, with significantly more Black females applying than males. This disparity creates challenges for college admissions offices trying to build a balanced incoming class. One challenge is how to increase the number of Black males applying to college; another challenge is avoiding the collateral damage that can happen when Black female applicants are not reviewed by the same standards as their male counterparts. Striving for gender balance, despite the Supreme Court's ruling, will remain a priority for most colleges and universities. This chapter looks at some of the dynamics that may influence why Black males are revered in selective college admissions in contrast to Black females.

Stephen A. Smith, a graduate of Winston-Salem State University in North Carolina and cohost of the popular show *First Take* on ESPN, often gives this response to an accusation that something was not fair: "Fair is a place where they judge pigs." While this sentiment could be applied to many parts of life, it could be no truer than in college admissions. Little about college admissions is fair, especially at selective colleges. As each year passes, application numbers continue to rise, with many application platforms allowing students to apply to multiple schools at one time; admit rates continue to go down as a direct result of the increase in applications; and college admissions decision-making becomes harder and harder for students, parents, and college counselors to understand. At many of the top schools in the country, there are far fewer spaces available than there are applicants, with admit rates being as low as 5 percent at schools such as Stanford and Harvard. That means that 95 percent of the students who applied to that school were denied admission. When asked about the competitive nature of admissions and the low admit rates, a dean at one of the nation's most selective institutions commented, "It's turning into a sweepstakes."

For schools that your family is considering, look up the gender balance of the student body, if that is a consideration in your college search.

When schools build their incoming class, they should ideally consider factors beyond grades, test scores, activities, essays, and courses taken. They factor in class size; institutional priorities such as gender balance, legacy applicants, athletic recruits, artistic contributors, and academic interest; and university priorities for educational, socioeconomic, geographic, and racial diversity. On top of all of this, schools must balance a financial aid budget. The more competitive a school is, the less fair the outcome is for most applicants.

When co-ed institutions form their first-year class, the goal for most is to get as close to a fifty-fifty gender balance as possible to achieve gender parity in the classroom and some semblance of fairness in the process. The reality, though, is that females outnumber males in college applicant pools. According to the National Student Clearinghouse, nearly 60 percent of the students in college in 2020–21 were women. This trend will probably continue, as there is also a decrease in the number of men enrolling in college. When you look at the gender difference among Black students, the balance becomes grossly lopsided, with often an 80 to 20 percent gender split among Black students. The disparity in gender at some HBCUs is much higher than at others with, for example, both Clark Atlanta University and Coppin State University having more than 75 percent female undergraduate enrollees. However, they are not alone, as many PWIs have a significant gender gap between male and female Black students, but these data are often not publicly reported. Thus, when it comes to admissions for Black female and male applicants, males would appear to have a decisive numbers advantage.

Coppin State University (HBCU)
Baltimore, MD
1,800 Undergraduates
Private
Graduate Students: Yes
Setting: Urban

There Are More Black Men in Jail Than in College

As Black males growing up in the 1980s and 1990s, we always heard the perpetuated myth that "there are more Black men in jail than in college." Few things in my life have had the duality of being simultaneously great and frustrating as much as being a Black male. **Being a well-educated Black male has brought me praise, power, and position but also an acute awareness that all of it could be snatched away from me in a millisecond by someone who feels threatened by my color and gender**. All Black males in America deal with this in some way. Our parents, communities, and media often make us feel loved and revered as models of success in sports and entertainment. Still, too often we also learn to hate or undervalue ourselves. So much of what we see is hopelessness and despair that it can be impossible to ignore.

When we talk about Black males in the history of America, there is clearly a love-hate relationship. On one hand, Black men have long been revered as athletes, actors, civil rights leaders, and activists, but, on the other hand, they are often looked on as criminals and savages when viewed outside popular entertainment or politics. The idea of the Black man as an athlete is normalized, but a Black man who's an intellectual is something rarely seen. The reality, though, is that Black men have a far better chance of reaching long-term financial success with a college education or by entrepreneurship than they do of becoming a professional athlete.

An argument could be made that the most valuable group of people to higher education institutions is Black males. Consider the amount of revenue generated by college football and men's basketball through multibillion-dollar television contracts, which serve as the foundation of the National Collegiate Athletic Association (NCAA) and fund many of the other intercollegiate sports. In 2022 it was estimated that the NCAA generated almost 1.2 billion dollars in revenue, with Black males as the primary drivers behind it and March Madness accounting for most of those profits. As sought after as many young Black men are for their athletic talents, so too are the brightest Black males sought after at the top academic schools in the country for their academic abilities and the diversity they bring to campus. While there are many factors that go into recruiting for both athletics and academics, in both cases, the numbers don't lie. If you show a coach a football player who can run the 40-yard dash in 4.2 seconds or a basketball player with a 40-inch vertical jump who can shoot three-pointers, the coach is going to find it hard to pass on such rare ability. The same is true for a Black male with a 3.8 GPA and 1400 on the SAT or 34 on the ACT; not many schools are going to pass on that applicant either.

If you are a parent or guardian of a Black male, you are aware of the many challenges that Black males in America have faced through history and in the current climate. There has been much attention paid to the many deadly encounters between police and Black people in the past few years. Many Black parents have "the talk" early on with their sons and daughters about how they should conduct themselves when encountering the police. Although race will no longer be used in college admissions for the foreseeable future, the lived experiences and narratives of Black males will be more important than ever. It's good to know that the college search process is one of the rare situations in our society where Black males are held in high regard. Black males make up one of the smallest populations in most college applicant pools, with only Native and Indigenous students being fewer in most instances. Because Black males make up such a small portion of applicants for many universities and colleges, they have become a high priority in applicant pools, and finding ways they can stand out with their application essays is going to be especially important moving forward.

Enrollment managers look at the makeup of the applicant pool and notice the small portion of Black males, as well as the subset of that small portion who are admissible. And because an even smaller subset than that will wind up enrolling, this population becomes even more important for schools looking to compose diverse classes. Given the shortage of Black male applicants, you will see news stories about a Black male who's admitted to all the Ivies. While it's a great accomplishment for this applicant, it highlights the priority that so many schools give to this population. A student can attend only one college at a time, of course. There is a period of time following admissions known as "yield season," after acceptances have been sent out, when schools do all they can to get the top admitted students, not just Black students, to enroll. They pursue any number of methods, including fly-in programs that bring students from across the country to their campus to experience campus culture and hear pitches about academic programs, competitive financial aid packages and scholarships, and other incentives. Schools want these admitted students to enroll so that the schools can achieve their institutional priorities.

It's important to note that the Supreme Court's ruling on race-conscious admissions in 2023 only restricts how colleges can evaluate and admit students. There are no restrictions on how colleges can recruit students or how they aim to achieve yield.

By no means are we saying that Black males are guaranteed admission by reason of simply applying, but they do occupy a unique place in higher education admissions by reason of their scarcity. I (Tim) can remember more than once coming across a Black man with a highly competitive application who was referred to as a "unicorn" in the applicant pool. You will hear coaches talk about a once-in-a-lifetime athlete who will change the game; well, that same conversation goes on in admissions offices throughout the country as well. **In both academics and athletics, postsecondary education puts a premium on Black males, but it is important that we define their needs and put their life success ahead of the needs of institutions that have not historically created spaces to support their identity and personal growth.**

Black Girl Magic

Black males are, unfortunately, scarce in most college applicant pools; Black females, on the other hand, make up the majority of Black applicants in those same pools. By the numbers, Black female applicants have better grades, test scores, extracurricular involvement, and application essays than Black males do. This is a sweeping generalization, we know, but there is an abundance of Black females competing in selective college admissions at the top universities in the country. But this is nothing new; we all know that the foundation of Black America was built on the shoulders of Black women such as Harriet Tubman and Sojourner Truth and, in a later era, Shirley Chisholm (Brooklyn College) and

Brooklyn College (PWI)
Brooklyn, NY
11,000 Undergraduates
Public
Graduate Students: Yes
Setting: Urban

University of Denver (PWI)
Denver, CO
5,400 Undergraduates
Private
Graduate Students: Yes
Setting: Urban

Condoleezza Rice (University of Denver). It was a great moment when Barack Obama was elected the first Black president of the United States, but where would he have been without Oprah? And some would argue that Michelle is the more popular and revered Obama. The Black women who have made an impression on all facets of this country are countless, and recently there have been no bigger names than Vice President Kamala Harris and Stacey Abrams.

Black women are the most educated population in the workplace, outpacing all other groups. Yet, on average, they are paid 35 percent less than white men and 15 percent less than white women, which gives truth to the saying "you have to work twice as hard to get half as far." As troubling as this is, there is an initiative by the company Goldman Sachs to help reduce disparities in pay. The company is making a ten-billion-dollar investment to address racial and gender bias in the workplace, with Black women being a major focus. This is good news for Black female college graduates who will be entering the workforce in the upcoming years, but the challenges for Black females begin long before that. They have one of the hardest challenges getting into the most selective schools in the country because they make up most of the applicant pool's Black students.

With around four thousand colleges and universities in the country, there are plenty of opportunities for young Black women to get a great education. But suppose your daughter is looking to attend any of the most selective colleges. In that case, it's going to take some "Black Girl Magic" to get in. Your daughter may have a 4.0 GPA, great test scores, and all the other accomplishments that make for a competitive candidate, but so will many other young Black females who'll apply. This is why you must ask questions during the college search: What makes my daughter special? What makes her different from other young women like her? What can she contribute to the school's community? And what school is going to appreciate what she has to offer?

In my more than twenty years in higher education, one of the hardest conversations I (Tim) ever had was telling one of my closest friends that her daughter was "regular" in the context of a selective college applicant pool. My friend shared with me all of her daughter's achievements with a great deal of pride, and they were truly great accolades; but the reality was that, in a selective college applicant pool, she would be put on a waitlist at best. At many other schools she would be a clear admit, but my friend wanted her daughter to go to a top-tier school, and in those schools' applicant pools, she would be just another "smart Black girl." This is disappointing and frustrating for all of us, but thankfully I was able to have this difficult conversation with her given our close friendship.

We want to make sure that the parents of daughters know this about the college admissions process: the numbers are not on their daughters' side in the way they are for sons. I (Tim) try to wrap my mind around this dynamic each day as I raise my twin son and daughter. They are just nine years old now, but it's obvious to see that, as with most children this age, my daughter "just gets it" while my son, equally as bright, gets the "he's a boy" pass, which many boys get throughout adolescence. Yes, I want both to strive for their best, but I must also deal with the reality of a society and educational world that will judge them differently, and I have already begun to teach them that "life is not fair." When we started in the profession, we had the naïve idea that the kids who were the smartest were the ones that were admitted, but over the past twenty-five years, we have witnessed firsthand that this is simply not true; the college admissions process is layered and has many nuances that make it difficult to understand from the outside looking in.

CHAPTER 11

Sports, Arts, and Special Talents

Overview

All of our beautiful Black children are gifted. Whether they have talent in the arts, athletics, sciences, math, technology, or a host of other things, we know for sure that they are not just numbers on a transcript. Oftentimes our children are interested in attending a college that will augment their gifts. We all know that many Division I and II college athletes do not pay full tuition for their education. Especially in football and basketball, scholarships are offered to high school students who, a school believes, will help it win games. This chapter provides an overview of how college admissions works for students with recruitable talent that may yield a scholarship. We discuss some do's and don'ts for students who hope to be recruited for the arts or athletics.

If your child has talent in the visual or performing arts, they belong to a distinctive group of college applicants. As a parent, you have helped them hone their craft, probably spending loads of money on materials and lessons as well as sacrificing tremendous amounts of time. Now your child must decide if this craft they've developed will help them get into college and if they want to major in the arts.

To be considered a candidate in the arts, applicants frequently have to create a portfolio of work or prepare for an audition. For students to show their best work, they must know what to do and when to do it. Whether their talent is in music, dance, drama, studio art, or computer animation, what is critical are timing, research, and preparation.

Is Your Child Considering an Art School or Conservatory?

If your child's ambition is to create art or perform for a living, then an art-intensive program is definitely the way to go. If, however, your child sees their art as a way to help them get into a school, but they (or you) are hesitant to commit to an art major, then maybe they should instead join a club, band, theater group, or use the studios available at the college they attend. Just as you would if your child were being recruited for athletics, you need to research the programs, professors, facilities, local venues, and internships available at schools of interest. One important question to ask is, What kind of degree should your child get? There are multiple possibilities: a BA (bachelor of arts), a BFA (bachelor of fine arts), or a BM (bachelor of music). There is no one degree that works for everyone.

What Are Visual and Performing Arts Departments Looking For?

When it comes to recruiting art students, here are three things that almost always hold true:

1. Colleges want to see a student's current ability and range to determine if they have the potential to succeed in an art program.
2. Art programs want to see a student's individual style and creativity.
3. Admissions officers and faculty members for the visual and performing arts do consider grades and test scores; they just don't weigh them as heavily as they do the portfolio or audition. Do not let your child think that their grades do not matter, however. What admissions officers are looking for are artistic talent and dedication *and* a solid academic record.

Can My Child Get a Scholarship for
Music, Dance, or Visual Art?

There are absolutely scholarships available to students in the arts. Many public and private colleges offer merit aid for students who will contribute to the artistic life of campus. However, to be clear, this can only happen if the student majors in the art. This cannot be a hobby if you expect scholarship money to be attached to it.

How Should My Child Prepare a
Portfolio or for an Audition?

Nothing is more important than knowing the requirements and deadlines for each college. Each school has strict guidelines that applicants must follow. The earlier that students start to gather artwork or record performances, the less rushed they will feel when it's time to present to a college. There are even "national portfolio days" when students and parents can meet with schools to present a student's work, and the student may get an offer of admission that day.

When your child is considering a performing arts school, you should evaluate it based on certain criteria. Here are a few questions to consider:

1. Is the school a conservatory or a university?
2. What majors are offered (a BFA or BA degree)?
3. How are the facilities (studios, practice rooms, equipment)?
4. Who are the key faculty members in the discipline of interest?
5. What art events happen at the school that your child would like to take part in?
6. Can your child pursue a double major or a major and minor in another department?
7. What is your child's specific area of interest within music, visual arts, dance, or theater? There are few generalists; most students who receive scholarships specialize in one area.

Does Your Child Want to Play a Sport in College?

In the last chapter, Tim wrote about Black men being the most valued asset on a college campus, oftentimes because of their participation in sports. Black men dominate in college football and college basketball. As I (Shereem) write this, I am thinking about Sam "Bam" Cunningham, who passed away in fall 2021. For those who do not know who he was, he was a running back at the University of Southern California and later in the NFL. Notably, Sam was a part of USC's "all Black" backfield—the first one of its kind in Division I (NCAA) history—that included quarterback Jimmy Jones and running back Clarence Davis. Sam had a remarkable debut performance (135 yards, two touchdowns) against an all-white University of Alabama football team, as USC beat Alabama 42 to 21 in Birmingham on September 12, 1970. Sam's performance in the game was reportedly a factor in convincing the University of Alabama and its fans to let Coach Bear Bryant integrate southern football. Jerry Claiborne, a former Bryant assistant, said, "Sam Cunningham did more to integrate Alabama in 60 minutes than Martin Luther King Jr. did in 20 years."

University of Alabama (PWI)
Tuscaloosa, AL
31,000 Undergraduates
Public
Graduate Students: Yes
Setting: Remote

We are all aware of the prominence of sports culture in America, and many of our Black children think of elite athletes as heroes and aim to emulate them on the field or on the court. Many affluent Black families owe their wealth to athletics. Whether athletics helped them get into college or they played a sport professionally, these Black athletes were smart with their money and used it as a foundation for wealth building. No one hates more than I do the assumption, which some people believe, that we were bred to be superior athletes through slavery. The notion that Blacks should "just dribble" or that we're so athletic but never cerebral infuriates me. However, it is a perception that is pervasive, and it passes down to our children, who are often praised, by us and others, for their athletic prowess more than their academic achievements.

I am a sports-obsessed dad who is fortunate to have a son who is equally as sports-obsessed. As a left-handed pitcher at the age of fifteen, he was offered a scholarship to play baseball by the University of North Carolina at Chapel Hill. Given what I saw as his potential as early as twelve years old, I knew he could play college baseball, and I have always encouraged his aspiration to play professionally. As a college advisor, I became keenly aware of how college recruiting for athletics works, how early it begins, and what we should do to help our children succeed. I added to my company's team an advisor who specializes in college sports recruiting.

Something happened, though, that changed my outlook. My son was asked to decommit from the team after a year and a half of belonging to the 2022 recruiting class at UNC–Chapel Hill. The school called him, not me, and told him that, due to COVID-19, there were too many kids on the team for him to play as a freshman. This was hard for a sixteen-year-old to hear but was even harder for me as a father to comprehend. The school didn't call me. It didn't call his high school coach. It called a child, and it was right then that I understood how cutthroat and cruel college recruiting can be.

I won't dwell on my disappointment but want instead to share what I learned. I know many other parents who trusted a coach's word and were then dropped unexpectedly. It happens to athletes of all colors. Thankfully, my son landed on his feet. If UNC had recruited him, then he would be recruited by another Power Five or equally strong program. But his rejection by UNC demonstrates how athletes are commoditized and expendable. If you want your child to be recruited or, better yet, if your child believes they have the talent to be recruited, you need to have your child evaluated by a credible coach or at a prospect camp or a showcase. Your child doesn't need to attend every single camp or showcase—they can get expensive—but you need to market your child if college coaches are trying to engage with them. The adage "if you're good enough, they will find you" is true in most cases, but as a parent involved in your child's college search, you'll want to identify what schools are best for your child athletically, academically, and socially. We should not jump hastily on the first opportunity that someone presents to us; instead we should survey the landscape and consider schools' cultures and how an experience and degree from a school will benefit our child.

Let me describe some possible steps to take for a family that's considering athletic recruitment as part of the admissions process.

Reclassing

Reclassing, or reclassifying, is holding a child back a year in middle school or high school so that they'll have an edge athletically by being taller, stronger, or more skilled than their peers. Parents are usually the ones who take the initiative in reclassing their child. Schools vary in their rules about whether an administrator has to sign off to permit a child to repeat a grade. But even when a principal has the right of refusal and doesn't allow reclassing, determined parents can take matters into their own hands and simply switch schools. Some have done just that.

> "It's not because a kid is not doing well in school or is too young for his grade. It's just because you'll be one year older in high school, and you'll be that much better of a player." (Bob Hurley, Hall of Fame basketball coach and head coach at St. Anthony's School in New Jersey)

Although my son did not reclass, despite being told that it would benefit his athletic development, I want more Black parents to be aware of reclassing. This practice is widespread for baseball among white families. Some call it "cheating"; others say it's the best and sometimes only way to get a Division I athletic scholarship. Many elite athletes in all sports are nineteen or twenty years old when they enter college. This is because they reclassed. It is a strategy that you should consider with some professional counsel from a coach or advisor you trust.

Schools Other Than Division I

Do not let ESPN make you think that the only students who get athletic scholarships play in the Power Five conferences (SEC, ACC, Pac-12, Big Ten, and Big 12). Plenty of HBCUs, Division II, and schools in the NAIA (National Association of Intercollegiate Athletics) offer athletic scholarships as well. Division III and Ivy League schools do not offer athletic scholarships, but they can recruit students and be creative with financial aid if they want an athlete badly enough. That's a secret they will not tell you in an information session.

Have a Resume and Video of
Your Child's Accomplishments

Make it easy for a recruitment coordinator to evaluate your child. If you share a resume and video (not only a highlight reel) with a coordinator, they have the choice to look at it or not. Many will discard it because they get so many of them, but someone will review it, and that person may want to recruit your child. Please encourage your child to go to a school where they are wanted—and will play—instead of where they will get the most initial recognition on social media.

Do Not Overlook HBCUs

Thankfully, and primarily due to Deion Sanders at Jackson State University, many elite high school athletes are rethinking what's important to them and are not just going where history has told them is the pathway to the pros. Many of the greatest NFL players—Shannon Sharpe (Savannah State), Jerry Rice (Mississippi Valley State University), Walter Payton (Jackson State University), and Steve McNair (Alcorn State University)—played football at HBCUs. We would be remiss if we did not also highlight celebrated sports journalist Pam Oliver, Florida A&M graduate, who has been covering the NFL and other sports for more than twenty years and has worked closely with many of the greats. Many great NBA players came from HBCUs as well: Ben Wallace (Virginia Union University), Charles Oakley (Virginia Union University), and Anthony Mason (Tennessee State University). Identifying what school, whether it is a PWI or an HBCU, is going to give your child the best chance to realize their dreams is what should drive the college search process. I am a strong believer that HBCUs, especially for football and basketball, should be considered for young men who have aspirations of playing professionally.

Fun fact about Tim: He earned a cross-country and track scholarship while at Morehouse that he did not have when he matriculated. He made the team as a walk-on and proved himself to be such a valuable contributor to the team that he was offered scholarship money as an athlete for his sophomore, junior, and senior years, winning multiple championships along the way. Isn't that cool!

Savannah State University (HBCU)
Savannah, GA
3,000 Undergraduates
Public
Graduate Students: Yes
Setting: Midsize City

Mississippi Valley State University (HBCU)
Bena, MS
1,700 Undergraduates
Public
Graduate Students: Yes
Setting: Remote

Alcorn State University (HBCU)
Lorman, MS
2,700 Undergraduates
Public
Graduate Students: Yes
Setting: Remote

Contact Coaches

"A closed mouth can't get fed." That saying is true in business and in college recruiting. If your child wants to attend a certain school, they must reach out to it. There are recruitment questionnaires online to fill out, and there are opportunities for students to take the initiative to connect with coaches. Given how much time an athlete spends with a team and its coach, many athletes choose the coach more than they choose the school. Of course, coaches may leave for a new job, but do not underestimate how important a coach is to your child's college recruitment and college experience.

Should Parents Reach Out to Coaches?

I have reached out to coaches and introduced myself when I think my son may be a good fit for a school. When I have allowed my son to be the sole contact with a coach, I have kicked myself: coaches have an agenda, and I will no longer allow my child—he's not eighteen years old and he's still on my dime—to navigate adult situations alone. Some people may disagree with this approach, and some coaches may be turned off by parental involvement. But I am a kind and courteous person, and I want to see if someone that I may entrust with my son is kind and courteous as well.

Many Black parents want their student-athletes to play at the highest level they can and to be funded to do so. There are some myths out there about athletic scholarships that we need to address.

Myth: Athletic scholarships are full rides offered in the senior year of high school.

Not true. In fact, most athletic scholarships are partial (or equivalency) scholarships, as each team's coach has a limited number of scholarships to offer each entering class. Other than football and basketball—the biggest athletic money generators for most institutions—only Division I tennis, gymnastics, and volleyball can offer full-ride scholarships for athletics. In recruiting athletes, a college coach can make a verbal offer as early as middle school, but it usually happens during freshman, sophomore, or junior year of high school, depending on the sport and the athlete's ability.

Please note the word *verbal*. In marital wedlock, vows matter, but a signed marriage certificate matters more. Students need to sign a National Letter of Intent to be officially committed to a school, and that happens during senior year. In our social media–driven world, too much is made of offers and verbal commitments. Do not believe that recruitment is secured until the ink is dry on the signed letter.

Myth: Talented athletes can get into any school even if their grades are poor.

Unfortunately, there is some truth to this one. Athletes are not held to the same admissions expectations at many elite universities, but your son or daughter should not think they can get Cs and Ds in high school and then get into college with no problem. Recruitment depends on how much a coach wants them and will push for them in the admissions process. By the same token, a coach can look at a student's GPA and test scores and immediately be turned off given the seeming lack of effort or ability. Coaches want to invest in student-athletes who will do well in the classroom and graduate. They can then boast about that fact to the parents of their next recruit. I urge you not to let your child get lackadaisical in the classroom. Grades, test scores, character, and effort all matter. In some cases, including my son's, his test scores helped to boost his athletic scholarship offer because the coach pulled from other university funding sources adjacent to the athletic scholarship's allotment.

Coaches Need to Keep Their Promises

I don't want to paint a negative picture of all college coaches, but I want you to heed the warning in what happened to my son. Coaches' loyalty lies with themselves and their athletic program, not with your child. As happens frequently in college football, coaches leave schools, or are fired, with little warning and perhaps with little regard for who else is affected. Now your child must impress a new coach who did not recruit them. This is a troubling but real possibility. When coaches make offers to student-athletes, they often make more offers than they need to, knowing that every kid they offer a scholarship to may not choose their program. This form of over-recruiting by coaches makes recruitment risky for families. The best advice I can give on this is to ask any and every question you have. Try to get to know the coach's character. You are trusting another adult to help shepherd your child into adulthood. You need to partner with this person, and they need to be a contact in your phone. You need to make sure everyone is on the same page. I am not talking about a promise of playing time; I am talking about learning what the coach believes in, what their team's graduation rate is, and what former student-athletes are now doing with their lives. Most of all you, the parent, need to be confident that this person can be an additional life coach for your child.

I have shared the story of my son's mistreatment in athletic recruitment with audiences at events where Tim and I promoted the book's first edition. Tim often told those in attendance that what they get in the book is the PG edit of an earlier draft where I went "HAM" on what I perceived to be racism. I have learned, though, that many student-athletes—Black, Brown, and white—get a raw deal in recruiting.

Superlative student-athletes may think they got offered a scholarship at a dream school, and once they verbally "commit" and put on the "engagement ring" to attend said school, even posting about the match on social media, they then "go off the market," so no other schools can recruit them. The harsh truth, though, is that no college has to keep its promise to a student-athlete. A student-athlete can get cut from the team before they even get to campus (yes, in July) or, even worse, get cut in the fall of their first year when they thought they were on the team of a spring sport. This late-date drop will send them scrambling to transfer to another school. It's exhausting and unfair, but collegiate sports are big business.

What Is the NCAA's Transfer Portal?

The NCAA's Transfer Portal is an online database that allows student-athletes to explore transfer options and communicate with coaches at other schools who may be interested in recruiting them. It was created by the NCAA to simplify the transfer process and give student-athletes more control over their collegiate athletic careers.

The Transfer Portal has both positive and negative effects on student-athletes. One advantage of the portal is that it helps them move to another school if they think they aren't getting enough playing time where they are or want to play for a more competitive program. This can be particularly beneficial for athletes looking to increase their chances of being drafted to play professionally. On the other hand, the Transfer Portal can have negative effects. For example, it can create instability in college sports programs, as athletes may change schools suddenly, leaving coaches with little time to recruit replacements.

The portal has been a source of controversy since its inception, with some people arguing that it has made it too easy for student-athletes to switch schools and thus hinders a coach's ability to build a stable program. In recent years, there has been an increase in the number of student-athletes using the Transfer Portal, which has led some to claim that its use is getting out of control.

The effects of the Transfer Portal on HBCUs are mixed. On the one hand, HBCUs may benefit, as it could help them attract superior athletes who are looking for a change of scenery or are not getting as much playing time as they would like. Having this additional avenue for recruitment could make HBCUs more competitive in college sports and, in turn, attract more attention and funding to their athletic programs. On the flip side, the Transfer Portal could also have negative effects on HBCUs. It could drain talent from HBCUs, if athletes looking to transfer prefer to play for a larger or better-known school than the HBCU they currently attend. Since HBCUs generally have fewer resources than large PWIs, they may have a hard time attracting high-performing transfers or retaining talented student-athletes who find other opportunities through the portal. This could widen the gap between HBCUs and other institutions in their athletic success and make it more difficult for HBCUs to secure funding for their athletic programs.

In general, the Transfer Portal can be a useful tool for student-athletes who want more control over their academic and athletic careers. They must carefully consider, however, the potential consequences of transferring schools and work closely with their coach and academic advisor to make an informed decision about it.

Other Special Talents

Instead of arts *or* athletics, why not combine the two and get recruited? Colleges can offer scholarships for marching band and cheerleading, which support the athletic programs. The recruiting process for cheerleading is a little different from recruitment for other sports because it isn't a sanctioned NCAA sport, meaning that there are no established regulations around coach contact or recruiting calendars. Therefore, coaches and recruits can communicate and express interest at any time.

The key to earning most marching band scholarships is to be admitted to the school and, once admitted, to make the band. If your child is interested in a particular school, see if the school has a summer band camp. This experience can improve their skill at performing, raise their profile as a marching band performer, and give them a feel for the school's band and its band director.

We must continue to celebrate our children for all their gifts and use their gifts to get funding for college. Money is probably the greatest obstacle to all Black children getting a college education. Historically, the arts and athletics have helped us fund what we all deserve. We encourage you to help your child maximize their potential for whatever they aspire to be and to identify colleges and scholarships, for athletics or arts, that ultimately best suit their needs.

CHAPTER 12

Show Me the Money

Overview

College is expensive; there is no way around it. As families begin to think about college, funding an education should be at the forefront of the conversation. Financial aid offers will vary for each family. We do not get into the granular aspects of how aid packages are created because that is not our area of expertise; instead, we provide an overview of what families need to know as they think about how to fund their child's education. We also define financial aid terms.

———

Getting into college is one thing, but paying for college is a completely different challenge, especially given the continuing rising cost of tuition. When it comes to financial aid, students and families echo the words of Cuba Gooding Jr.'s character in *Jerry Maguire*— "Show me the money!" Paying for higher education is like taxes: everyone is going to have to pay some amount for college, but how much someone will pay depends on many factors.

At most colleges and universities, the financial aid process is separate from the admissions process. It is also more complex than most people realize. Federal, state, and institutional aid award amounts are determined and overseen by formulas. Oftentimes financial aid professionals can explain the formulas, but they have little control over how much money is allocated to students. Some financial aid packages are filled with loans instead of merit aid and grants. Why? Because most colleges cannot afford to meet 100 percent of all students' actual need.

Federal direct student loans are entitlements that allow US citizens and those with a Permanent Resident Card to borrow funds for college costs from the US Department of Education. These loans do not require credit checks or a creditworthy cosigner, which makes them relatively easy to get but also dangerous. We encourage families to read the fine print of a loan's terms and try to understand them as best they can. Many of us do not see loans as a form of financial aid because they have to be repaid. That is why students need a plan in place for getting a job after graduation that will let them begin repaying their loans as quickly as possible.

We would advise everyone to apply for financial aid, no matter how well off your family is. If you don't apply for aid, there is little to no chance of receiving anything. We often hear from families who were told or who assume they would not qualify for financial aid given how much money they make. There are schools that award aid for reasons other than need and merit; if students don't have an aid application on file, however, they are not considered for some of these additional funding opportunities.

Another important reason for families to apply for aid is the fact that you never know what may happen to your finances. Having been in higher education through a recession and a global pandemic that affected almost all families financially in some way, we have witnessed firsthand how colleges and universities were able to step in and supplement funding for students who had aid applications on file. We encourage all families to apply for aid, but ultimately applying is a personal decision. Please note that requirements vary from school to school, but many schools are going to require most, if not all, of the forms and documentation we describe later in the chapter. **Always remember: the college or university is the best resource for information about the financial aid process for your child.**

> Adhere to *all* deadlines. Deadlines are one of the most important parts of the admissions process. Missing them can cost your student the chance to apply to schools as well as access to financial aid.

Without timely submission of financial aid information, students will be unable to receive an aid package. Thus, it is imperative that parents and guardians submit all aid documents by the deadlines because in many instances financial aid, especially institutional, is awarded on a first-come, first-served basis. If you miss deadlines, often the remaining amount of aid available will be limited. We cannot impress upon families and guardians enough the importance of submitting aid documents ahead of deadlines.

Preparing to Pay for College

There are steps you should take as early as possible in preparation for funding your child's education:

Begin talking about money as early as possible. Having candid family conversations about the cost of higher education is critical. Both parents and student need to manage expectations around college choices based on the family's income and savings.

Consider the option of opening a 529 savings plan. A 529 plan is a tax-advantaged savings plan designed to encourage saving for future education costs. These plans, legally known as "qualified tuition plans," are sponsored by states, state agencies, or educational institutions and are authorized by section 529 of the Internal Revenue Code. By opening a 529 savings plan, you will be able to save money toward your child's college education, and you will also receive some tax deductions in most states. You can also use your 529 assets for K–12 tuition up to $10,000 per student per year at a public, private, or religious school. If this is of interest to you, contact your accountant or tax professional.

A provision of the SECURE 2.0 Act, passed by Congress in late 2022, now allows a beneficiary of a 529 savings plan to deposit its distributions in a Roth IRA (individual retirement account) owned by the same beneficiary. The 529 account must have existed, been contributed to, and owned by the beneficiary for fifteen years in order to move funds from it into a Roth IRA. The lifetime limit for tax- and penalty-free rollover is $35,000.

Use a net price calculator (NPC). Net price calculators are available on colleges' and universities' websites. They allow prospective students to enter information about themselves to find out what students like them paid to attend the institution the previous year, after taking grants and scholarship aid into account. If the NPC determines there's a difference in the cost of the school and what your family can pay, you will need to apply for aid and review the information we provide in the remainder of this chapter.

Be prepared to pay something. A full scholarship by which a family pays no money at all for their student to attend college for four years is rare. Even if your child does receive a scholarship, you should have some money set aside for incidental costs and emergencies.

Be prepared to apply for aid annually. Your family will have to go through this process every year that your student is enrolled in college.

Financial Aid 101

Applying for financial aid today is not the same process that it was for those of us who went to college decades ago. More than likely you will never touch a piece of paper. Everything today is digital. Your child will probably not have to wait for hours to see a financial aid counselor; in fact they may never meet their financial aid counselor. There is so much about the process that has changed, but there are a lot of things that have stayed the same. Below are some terms you need to know.

Applying for Aid

There are two applications you will need to complete if you are applying for financial aid:

FAFSA (Free Application for Federal Student Aid). The FAFSA is a form that current and prospective college students complete in the United States to determine their eligibility for student financial aid. The FAFSA is different from the CSS Profile, which some colleges also require. Students must submit this form to be eligible for federal financial aid, including grants, loans, and work-study. Parents should help students complete it to ensure the accuracy of the information since it is the dominant financial resource for college students. There is a federal method for determining the Student Aid Index (SAI), which was formerly called the expected family contribution, or EFC. The SAI is a calculation of a family and student's financial need in paying for higher education. The FAFSA will open near the end of the calendar year, around December. A student should plan to submit the application soon after it opens in the student's twelfth-grade year. As its name suggests, this is a *free* application, so you should never pay to submit it. Not long ago, the FAFSA was simplified; the number of questions on the form was reduced from over one hundred to around forty.

Other updates to the FAFSA were made as well. For families that own a farm or small business, the FAFSA has new requirements for disclosure, and the income from it will figure in the determination of a family's capacity to pay college expenses. This means that some families may not qualify for as much financial aid as they would have before. Families with more than one student enrolled in college at the same time will no longer receive a discount. Previously, if a family's contribution was $20,000, and the family had two children enrolled in college in the same year, that figure was divided by two and so equaled $10,000 for student 1 and $10,000 for student 2. Now, both students 1 and 2 will each have the same contribution of $20,000 to make. Institutions will have discretion, though, in how they handle financial awards for students whose families are paying to send more than one child to college in the same year.

CSS Profile. The College Board's CSS Profile is an online application that collects information used by hundreds of colleges, universities, professional schools, and scholarship programs to award financial aid from sources outside the federal government. It is found on the College Board's website (www.collegeboard.org) and is often required in addition to the FAFSA. Unlike the FAFSA, the CSS Profile charges a fee per submission to an institution, although waivers of this fee are available to an applicant whose family makes below a certain annual income. Each college has a different method for calculating financial need. This application must be filed in October of a student's senior year. This application will primarily be required by private and some larger public schools to help award merit and non-federal aid. Currently, more than four hundred schools require this additional application. The reason that schools ask for this additional application is to have a better understanding of the resources available to support students when the schools are giving out millions of dollars in institutional aid.

When you complete these forms, you will need to have your tax return prepared and available. With any financial aid application, tax returns are necessary for documenting finances. Recent updates to aid regulations allow families to use prior year tax returns, meaning they can use 2021 tax returns if applying for aid in 2023, but up-to-date tax returns are more helpful for schools trying to put together the best aid package. Don't worry about needing any paper copies. Technology has made it possible to have your most recent tax returns sent to the school directly from the federal government without leaving the FAFSA or CSS Profile sites.

Another important part of financial aid is having a complete understanding of your family's financial situation. Financial aid offices are aware that there are families where parents are divorced or where students are in foster care or where a student's guardians have died. No matter the situation, it is critical that all adults who provide financial support to a college-bound student furnish tax documents to financial aid offices.

One request that an aid office often makes is for submission of a non-custodial waiver form. This form allows families to provide additional information about a parent or guardian who does not live with the student to determine if tax information from that individual can be waived. Aid offices will make that determination in such instances.

The FAFSA, CSS Profile, and your tax documents are used to determine your family's demonstrated/calculated financial need. To calculate your family's demonstrated need, the school will take the cost of attendance and subtract from it your family's Student Aid Index.

Student Aid Index (SAI). Determined by the FAFSA using the federal method and reported to the family in the Student Aid Report. The SAI determines need-based federal and state aid as well as aid from many colleges. The SAI represents how much need-based financial aid a student is eligible for in a given year. Merit and need-based aid do not reduce the SAI.

Cost of attendance (college sticker price). The direct billable costs (tuition and fees, room and board) and indirect costs (books, supplies, personal expenses). This can vary from family to family depending on spending habits.

Most colleges do not meet 100 percent of demonstrated financial need, creating a gap, which is the pressure point for many families in paying for college. Once your demonstrated need is determined, a financial award offer is put together for your student. In this award, financial aid comes in four primary forms: scholarships (need-based and merit-based), grants, work-study, and student loans. Let's define each.

Merit-based scholarships. These are awarded for achievements and skills, including academic excellence, athletic or artistic ability, or volunteer service. This type of scholarship is often awarded immediately following high school or during college. There are multiple resources to learn about scholarships, and we suggested some in the introduction. We also recommend that you read *The Ultimate Scholarship Book* by Gen and Kelly Tanabe.

Need-based scholarships. These are awarded in cases of financial necessity. These scholarships are awarded according to a family's income, liabilities, savings, and assets.

Grants. These are funds given to your child that do not need to be paid back. Most grants are based on financial need calculated with the FAFSA; they come from the state or the federal government and are awarded through a college. Federal Pell Grants can be awarded in an amount over $5,000. Private and some public universities have additional institutional grants they can award apart from federal or state grants.

Work-study. This is a job your student is hired for at the college; they qualify for work-study employment through demonstrated need as determined by the financial aid office. Jobs can take place at many spots on campus, such as working in a library, a dining hall, or an administrative office. These jobs offer students a paycheck during college so they can have pocket money or put it toward their tuition bill. Work-study aid is a part of a financial award, but students must work to receive it.

Loans. Yes, we know *loan* is a four-letter word. For students and parents to take out loans is not ideal, but often it is necessary. The goal of taking out any loan should be an investment in a student's potential future earnings. The key is to borrow as little as possible— by parent or student—and to pay it back as quickly as possible. We do not recommend taking out private student loans because of the higher interest rates and because the expectation usually is that they will need to be paid back soon.

Below are some important terms to know when discussing loans:

Interest rate. An expense charged for borrowing money. The percentage of the interest rate varies.

Subsidized loan. A direct federal loan based on need. Interest does not accrue while a student is in college.

Unsubsidized loan. A direct federal loan not based on need. Interest does accrue while a student is in college.

Master Promissory Note. A legally binding contract you must sign when accepting any kind of federal loan. This outlines all the terms and conditions under which you agree to repay the loan.

Consolidation loan note. This combines all direct federal student loans into a single loan with one lender and one interest rate.

Parent PLUS loan. A direct federal loan to parents or graduate students that has a higher interest rate than undergraduate student loans.

Perkins Loan. A loan directly from a college rather than the federal government, one awarded for exceptional financial need.

We just covered a lot of terminology pertaining to financial aid. The reality is that financial aid is one of the most complicated parts of college admissions. Aid offices do all they can to provide as much financial support to students as institutional funding allows. When families begin the process of applying for financial aid, they must know the importance of submitting the appropriate documentation, meeting all deadlines, and following up with aid offices to complete the process. We would encourage families not to be defensive or secretive about submitting financial information, as aid offices are not asking for your financial information for any reason other than to provide the best aid package for your student. They want to *show you the money.*

Facts about the FAFSA and Financial Aid

Since the FAFSA collects the principal information for all financial aid awards, we offer you some facts that should help you complete it well.

1. The official FAFSA website is www.fafsa.ed.gov. ONLY USE THIS WEBSITE! You should *never* pay to complete the FAFSA.
2. Federal financial aid, like most state and university aid, is available on a first-come, first-served basis. The sooner you get your application in, the better your chances will be of qualifying. Deadlines are very important.
3. Accept money in this order:
   • Free money (scholarships and grants)
   • Earned money (work-study)
   • Borrowed money (loans)
4. After registering for the FAFSA, you will receive an FSA ID. This expires every eighteen months. Parents can use their FSA ID when completing the FAFSA application for multiple dependents.
5. Each FSA ID must be tied to a separate email address. Parents and child cannot use the same email address.
6. There is a tool called the IRS Data Tool that saves you time when filling out the FAFSA because tax information is taken directly from the IRS's database and populated in your FAFSA. You're less likely to make mistakes using this, and you will not need to manually gather your tax records before applying.
7. If a major life event impacts your finances, but is not reflected in your FAFSA (job loss, family illness, personal illness), contact the financial aid office at the schools to which your child is applying and have your records updated. Sometimes schools can make accommodations given the new circumstances.

8. When does a student *not* need their parents' financial information to qualify for federal or institutional financial aid?
   - If the student is twenty-four years or older by December 31 of the school year for which they are applying for financial aid
   - Is working toward a master's or doctorate degree
   - Is married
   - Is currently serving in the US military as active duty

Parents, before you pass judgment on student loans, ask yourself two questions about your own loans: (1) Would I be where I am in life without those loans? (2) Did I use those loans responsibly?

Let your answers frame how you see the use of loans in your child's higher education, if they are to be a part of your child's financial aid package.

PART III
Process

CHAPTER 13

The Power of Essay Writing

Overview

We firmly believe that application essays are now more important in college admissions than ever. Given the US Supreme Court's ruling in 2023 against affirmative action and the growing number of test-optional colleges and universities, students must write essays that *amplify their authenticity* to make their applications compelling.

———

Let me (Shereem) begin by clarifying something. When students and parents ask me about the *college essay*, what they usually mean is the personal statement. I'm quick to point out to them, however, that applications often require multiple essays. Most selective schools ask students to submit more than one piece of writing in the form of a *supplemental* essay or even two or three of them. Supplemental essays are designed to elicit further evidence of an applicant's qualifications beyond what they communicate in their personal statement. The focus of this chapter is primarily on the personal statement or essay, and it addresses parents and students, separately. Its goal is to answer some of the questions that are commonly asked about the college essay:

- What makes a college essay good?
- How can parents help students write a good one?
- Should an essay be about a student's race or culture?
- How can artificial intelligence assist with college essay writing?
- How does the personal statement differ from a supplemental essay?

Why are college essays important to me? Well, for starters, I love the written word. My third-grade teacher, when I was a student at Brooklyn Friends School, poured into me when I was an eight-year-old and encouraged me to be a writer. This led me to believe in my craft, and my educational pursuits at both Wesleyan University and Middlebury College's Bread Loaf School of English fortified my literary foundation. My love for writing is one of the primary reasons why I founded my company, Strategic Admissions Advice. Beyond building college lists and offering application strategies, I see my professional purpose as teaching students how to brainstorm and revise their essays.

Middlebury College (PWI)
Middlebury, VT
2,550 Undergraduates
Private
Graduate Students: Yes
Setting: Remote

In our book's first edition, we did not have a chapter specifically about college essays. We were remiss. After its publication, we received many questions from students and parents about college essays and their contribution to admissions decisions. Add to that the Supreme Court's ruling against affirmative action, and the self-revealing opportunity presented by the college essay became a vital topic even more deserving of its own chapter.

We think it paramount to take a vigorous approach in helping students craft a distinctive narrative about themselves in their applications. We know that some, not all, secondary schools and school counselors are protective and territorial about how they counsel students on writing college essays. Many independent schools have staff who conduct essay writing workshops or can afford to bring in a writing specialist to lead a lesson on composing the college essay. Most of these counselors or specialists are white and fail to consider, by no fault of their own (usually), that Black students have unique stories to tell: ones that need to be encouraged and expounded on in ways that can effectively support their applications.

Some Black students we speak to are often the "only" in their suburban public school or independent private school. Understandably, when they write their personal statement, many of them choose to describe their experience as an only, which makes sense to their supportive instructors. But that essay, the story of onlys, has been written before. It is diluted because it's not distinctive. If every Black student attending a private school writes about this "cultural fish out of water" phenomenon, what makes them different? Colleges already know that the well-funded secondary schools they come from are predominately white and can assume that a Black student may have faced some racial challenges along the way. But do those challenges necessarily identify who they are or who they're becoming? No. There's a fine line between wanting to tell an important story and rehashing a decades-long predicament that many Black students in white spaces have had. **The college essay is not a journal entry; it's a documented expression of identity that needs to separate its writer from any other student who ever applied to college. Ever.**

Yes, I am emphatically animated about this. I want students to shine with their essays, not blend in. More than that, I do not want students, especially Black students, to allow themselves to be stereotyped. This is a delicate topic to take up, I know, so I'll do it with a story.

Years ago, a family friend called me during the holidays on December 30, two days before the January 1 application deadline. I had previously given her some college admissions advice, informally, concerning her son, a senior in high school. Little did she know, the 30th was also my wedding anniversary; I shouldn't have been answering my phone that day, but I did, and I'm glad I did. This friend was a college-educated mom, an attorney, and a woman of Alpha Kappa Alpha Sorority. Her husband, a Kappa, was an entrepreneur. They had paid years of tuition for their son to attend an independent school. They fit the description of parents who would be involved and conscientious about college admissions, and they were. To an extent.

Well before this holiday phone call, the family had made a list of schools they felt good about, and the parents had given their son the autonomy to write his personal essay with the support of his school counselor. It is fair to assume this should have been enough. But then my friend finally read her son's personal statement two days before the deadline and was unsettled by it enough to call me. He had written his college essay about his love of basketball and hip-hop. This alarmed her because of its stereotypical connotations, and she wasn't sure why he would choose to write the all-important essay about how his most valuable life lessons came from these two interests. She asked me if I thought the essay was "good," and I was honest with her: this essay would not help him get into a selective college.

Two thoughts were dominant in my mind: (1) Why would he choose to write about either of these when, to my knowledge, he was not a recruited basketball player or had aspirations of becoming a hip-hop artist? And (2) who signed off on this essay and told him it was okay to submit?! A teenager applying to college for the first time does not know any better. A school counselor, on the other hand, especially one working at an independent school to which parents sometimes pay in excess of $25K a year, should have known better. Well-meaning parents often hand over the admissions reins to their child and the child's school counselor without being adequately informed and engaged. By the time I got the call, her son was up against the application deadline with a questionable essay that had his attorney mother, understandably, panicking.

I do not want the same thing to happen to your family.

How Can Parents Help with the Essay?

Please do not assume that your child knows what to write about or that their school counselor will read their essay well in advance and offer constructive criticism. Most critically of all, do not wait until the last minute to read your child's college essay. You might be thinking, "But it's their essay, right?" If so, then remind me: Whose money is paying for their education?

Writing a college essay (or essays, as mentioned above) is, in some ways, the culmination of the college admissions process. It involves identifying what's important to the writer (student, not the parent) and expounding on it in a distinctive way. It requires reflection, introspection, brainstorming, revising, and proofreading. To do this takes time.

For all students, regardless of color, writing a college essay means "telling your story." Like snowflakes, no two essays can be or should be the same. We each have a different life story, and in the essay or essays written for an application, students have a chance to reveal parts of themselves that aren't evident elsewhere in their application. Thus, the essay should be approached as an opportunity, a critical chance to relay a message not rooted in numbers, as are grades or scores, or expressed in another person's words, like letters of recommendation. The essay belongs to the student and the student alone. By the end of the writing process, regardless of the admission outcome, the student should have a magnus opus of which they are extremely proud.

So, what can a parent do to help? Assist with brainstorming at the beginning and proofreading at the end. That's it. Doing more in the middle will probably cause friction between you and your emerging young adult. Yes, they will need an adult to offer some suggestions along the way, but that should not be you. It should, ideally, be someone who has read application essays before—a school counselor or independent educational consultant—and probably *not* an English teacher. Hard truth: **college essays are very different from essays written for English class.** High school students are taught to write essays with a thesis, body paragraphs to support it, and a conclusion that revisits it in summary. That is not what a college essay should look like.

A college essay is a story. It's a slice of your child's life in which they share something important about who they are. It's not an autobiography of their entire seventeen or eighteen years on Earth but rather a sampling of an event when they learned something they believe will travel with them forever. This is why having your child draft their essays during the summer before senior year is so important. When students return to school as seniors, they'll be busy with classes, sports, clubs, performing arts, or socializing. Having completed, by Labor Day, a solid draft of the personal essay and any supplemental essays required for Early Decision or Early Action applications will feel like a huge weight has been lifted from them.

Many parents think that college essays are supposed to be about overcoming a hardship that other people haven't suffered. Hardship does not have to be the essay's subject, however. Here are some other topics to consider as you brainstorm with your child:

- cultural or familial traditions
- places that have special meaning for them
- a characteristic or trait they have that's rare
- a mantra or motto that keeps them going
- an experience of theirs that was positively transformative

Admissions officers are interested in learning more about an applicant as a whole person, and essays can provide valuable insights into their character and motivations. Essays can demonstrate an applicant's writing skill and other intellectual abilities. Admissions officers want to see evidence that an applicant can express their ideas effectively and coherently. Essays can reveal a student's knack for engaging with ideas and for thinking about them critically.

Parents, be a resource for your rising senior during the writing process or seek assistance from a professional.

Students: How to Write an Authentic and Awesome College Essay

Writing a college essay is hard. Students, I know you usually do not go into the writing process feeling "pumped" to sit in front of a computer to tell your own story. It's laborious, oftentimes frustrating, and occasionally embarrassing. It makes you extra critical and sometimes unable to recognize how talented as you are. Thinking about what's important to you and then revealing who you are to a stranger is weird and may feel uncomfortable. The most common thing I hear from students is "I don't know what to write!"

Know what's far easier to do? Documenting life. Instead of trying to devise some clever epiphany you hope will get you into the college of your dreams, share what has happened in your life in the past or what is happening now. Documenting is the key to storytelling. College essays are not supposed to be imaginative per se, but rather revealing. The way to be revealing is to

- tell your unique story,
- be real and authentic, and
- share details about something not already covered in the application.

The purpose of a college essay is to "introduce" yourself to a college admission officer in your own words. Most applicants will never meet the admissions officers who read their application file, so the essay is a chance for those unmet readers to hear directly from the applicant. This is why brainstorming, choosing the right topic, and having an opening line that "hooks" the reader is so important. With so much at stake for you, and your readers having so little time to spare, your essay's first paragraph must make them want to read on to learn more about you. I am a big believer in the power of opening lines. Here are some of my past favorites from students:

"Getting kicked in the mouth is not fun. Especially when receiving the kick from a Brazilian 5th-degree black belt who had been fighting to win a spot on his homeland's Olympic team."

"I have to break up with my twin sister. After seventeen years of being together, we need to go our separate ways."

*"I always talk to Uber drivers. Growing up, my mother
frequently reminded me that I should not talk to strangers.
However, I disagree."*

"I would rather sing than talk."

All of these opening lines make me want to read on. That's the goal: **intrigue the admissions officer, spark their curiosity, and share who you are.**

Remember that this is an exercise in documenting your life, not in creating a new story. Simply share—either what's going on now or what happened in the past to shape who you are today. Embrace the opportunity and let your fingers dance on the keyboard of your computer or your phone as you write. Or, if you find yourself frozen and unable to write anything, try recording yourself as you speak the ideas out of your head. You could even use voice typing, found under "Tools" in Google or "Dictate" in Microsoft Word, which transcribes what you say, accurately for the most part, and thereby gives you something to work with. (FYI I am writing this sentence by talking into my computer pretty cool huh.) You could also use artificial intelligence to help you brainstorm ideas and frame what you want to say. More on that below.

Writing a good college essay demands that you be honest and factual. Your essay will have a theme, not a thesis and topic sentences. Remember: you're writing a short story that documents a slice of your life. You are its protagonist—the main character or hero—and you're going to shine by drawing in the reader with imagery and details. Your goal is to share and evoke emotion. Revealing something about yourself is not easy, but doing so can make you stand out from other applicants.

Do not edit at any time while writing your first draft! No matter how much you write in your first go, whether it's two hundred words or eight hundred, you will by the end have produced something concrete, something that now exists outside your mind to look over, return to, and add to or alter. Any author will tell you that all first drafts are a mess. That's okay. What's important is getting something down on screen.

The Common Application requires the personal essay to be between 250 and 650 words. I encourage you to lean toward the maximum rather than the minimum. I honestly do not think I've ever read an amazing essay that was shorter than 500 words. Go for 650. Embrace the opportunity and write for quality *and* quantity.

Here are some more tips:

Be authentic. This means being brave enough to be truthful and vulnerable. Remember that you're documenting your truth. This is your story, not someone else's. Even if your story involves someone else, you're still the protagonist, and the focus should be on you. Once you've got the first draft out, read it aloud and ask yourself these key questions: Am I the focus of this story? Does this sound like me? Is this how I want to present myself?

Avoid repetition. Just as you shouldn't use words that don't sound like you, avoid repeating yourself, overusing words, and reusing cliches you have heard before. Vary your word choice, but be careful about it. Picking the longest or most exotic word from a thesaurus doesn't make you sound smart; it may backfire by making readers wonder if you wrote the essay yourself.

Tell a story. Stories are remembered. Don't tell the reader what happened; show them. Paint a picture for them so that they can "see" with your writing. Use emotion; make the reader understand how you felt in the moment and why.

Use appropriate language. The college essay isn't the place for slang, shorthand, or curse words you might use when texting a friend.

Follow directions and don't be too abstract. Admissions officers are not in your head when they read your essay. They're spending seven to twelve minutes reading your entire application. Being abstract or "cute" will not serve you well. Address the prompt when there is one and adhere to word limits.

Don't be careless. Typos and grammar mistakes will distract an admissions officer and are easily avoided. Spell-check and grammar-check your essays! This must be part of your proofreading. I recommend using a version of Grammarly, which checks for grammar, spelling, and typos and offers suggestions for awkward sentences or phrases.

Many mistakes are easy to make when drafting and are much easier to catch afterward when reading what you have already written. Below are some common mistakes to catch and fix when re-reading and editing your essays.

Homophones. These are words that sound the same but have a different meaning depending on their spelling. Spell checkers won't realize that you intended to write *pair* instead of *pare* or *pear*. Here's a list of problem-causing homophones:

your	you're	
their	they're	there
its	it's	
except	accept	
than	then	
week	weak	
to	too	two
who's	whose	
lessen	lesson	
hear	here	
forth	fourth	
buy	by	
board	bored	
affect	effect	
prejudice	prejudiced	

Incorrectly divided compounds or phrases. Spell checkers may not tell you that *can not* should be *cannot*, that *alot* should be *a lot*, and *inter net* should be *internet*, for example.

Usage errors. Most spell-check programs do not spot errors involving possession, such as the homophones *its* (possessive) versus *it's* (short for *it is*) or the plural nouns *children's* versus *kids'*.

Incorrect verb tenses. Spell checkers won't tell you when you've mixed up past and present verb tenses.

Should Students Write about Being Black?

Many colleges and universities value diversity, equity, and inclusion, despite the Supreme Court's 2023 decision, and they actively seek to create a diverse student body. Diversity includes having students on campus from different racial and ethnic backgrounds. So discussing your racial identity in a college essay could be relevant and meaningful.

In years past, there were unwritten rules about what content to avoid in college essays. Here are a few don'ts students have been told over the years:

1. Do *not* write about being in love or having a significant other. A college essay is not the place to talk about sex or how deeply you were moved or hurt by young love.
2. Do *not* use the essay to complain about your parents, teachers, or school. Teenage angst is tired, and no one wants to hear how badly people have treated you.
3. Do *not* write about politics or religion. These topics are too controversial, and you won't know your readers' beliefs about them or how they might react to yours.

Even today I am in full agreement with numbers 1 and 2. Relationships can change, and how you feel now may not be how you'll still feel months from now. But number 3 is not set in stone; we are living in a time in our country when once-taboo topics—politics and religion—are talked about openly on the news and in our daily lives and, dare I say, are unavoidable to discuss. This is not the time to be silent on these topics if there is something about them you're convinced you should say. When you open up about one of these topics, you are revealing your truth. If you choose to write about your racial identity as it relates to politics or religion in your college essay, it's important that you do so thoughtfully and with sensitivity.

Should Students Write about a Traumatic Event?

Whether to write about trauma in your college essay is a personal decision. Your college essay should not be the first time you share something you haven't told anyone before. There are pros and cons to writing about trauma in your college essay.

On the one hand, it can be a powerful way to connect with admissions officers and to show them who you are as a person. It can also be a way to find meaning in your trauma. On the other hand, writing about trauma might prove difficult and triggering for you. It might also be risky for your application, as admissions officers may not be prepared to read about so sensitive a topic. Admissions officers are not therapists, after all. It's important always to be respectful of yourself. Don't share anything you're not comfortable with sharing. And be mindful of your audience. If you're unsure whether to write about trauma in your college essay, talk about it with a trusted adult, such as a parent or counselor. They can help you to decide whether and how to go about it in a way that is safe and respectful of all parties involved.

Can Artificial Intelligence Assist in Essay Writing?

If you've been paying attention to education and technology news, you've likely heard about ChatGPT, the new tool from OpenAI that generates astonishingly humanlike text based on prompts and questions submitted by a user. We have gotten a lot of questions lately about how this tool should or should not be used when writing a college essay.

I am a firm believer that we have to lean into artificial intelligence as being a new tool at our disposal. AI can be a useful aid in writing college essays, but it is important to use it responsibly. ChatGPT can generate ideas and inspire essay writing by suggesting relevant topics to write about and prompting you to elaborate on them with supportive arguments and evidence. You can also use it to generate initial drafts of essays, which you can then revise and refine. But don't forget this: given the thousands of applications that more selective schools receive, the essay must be relevant to your lived experience. You should always infuse it with your own voice and perspective.

In my educational consulting business, I encourage students to use ChatGPT similarly to how they might record themselves or dictate to their phone or computer. I expect a proliferation of ChatGPT use by college applicants, so I am confident in saying that admission officers will soon develop hunches about which essays were auto-generated and which ones are authentic. As I write this, it's rumored that one school is going to add a question to its application asking applicants how they used AI to help them write their essays!

Here are some tips for using AI responsibly for writing college essays:

Brainstorming. ChatGPT can generate a range of ideas for your college essays based on your interests, experiences, and the essay prompts provided by institutions. After you enter information about yourself or pose a question, ChatGPT will generate topic suggestions that can kick-start your brainstorming.

Content development. Once you have a theme for your essay, ChatGPT can help you develop your essay's content by asking you probing questions to clarify your ideas and by providing suggestions for where to add evidence, examples, or anecdotes.

Organization and structure. ChatGPT can assist in organizing your thoughts and structuring your essay. You can discuss your ideas with ChatGPT and receive suggestions on how to structure your essay effectively, including tips on crafting a compelling introduction, developing coherent paragraphs, and creating a strong conclusion. This can help you create a well-organized and logically flowing essay that is easy for readers to follow.

Style and grammar. ChatGPT can provide suggestions for improving the grammar, syntax, and style of your college essays. It can flag and offer corrections to misspellings, grammatical errors, awkward sentence structures, and inconsistent writing style, which can help you polish your essays.

I am not so much advocating for ChatGPT as I am accepting that AI is here to stay and so shouldn't be dismissed without consideration. I recommend that you try using ChatGPT to generate ideas, to overcome writer's block if you encounter it, or to edit your writing, but the final essay must be your own work.

What Makes the Personal Statement Different from Supplemental Essays?

A personal statement is an essay required for applications to most colleges and universities. It is an opportunity for an applicant to introduce themselves to the admissions committee; share their background, interests, and achievements; and explain why they are a good fit for the college or university. Supplemental essays, on the other hand, are additional essays required by some colleges and universities to *supplement* the personal statement. The prompts for supplemental essays are tailored to the individual college or university. A prompt may ask applicants to explain why they want to attend that school specifically or how they would contribute to its community, or a prompt may pose another question of interest to the school. Which kind of essay, personal or supplemental, is more important to a "reach" school? The personal statement is typically the more important one, but students must look into a school's particular requirements for its application to understand what the school is likely to value in applicants' essays.

We are living in a time when, now more than ever, essays can play a pivotal role in an application being accepted or rejected. Colleges want to learn about who an applying student is and what's important to them. Students need to be proud of themselves, their good and bad life experiences, and be prepared to share who they are in an essay so that a school can make an informed decision about admitting them. Regardless of the admission decision to come, writing a college essay can document a truth or an aspiration that will advance a young person's self-understanding and propel them toward achieving greatness in the future.

CHAPTER 14

Expectation-for-Success Timeline

Overview

In this chapter, we discuss when the college search should begin, areas to focus on as your family puts your college list together, and important things to consider to limit anxiety. In college admissions, there is a context for why we do what we do and things that are necessary to understand in order to succeed during the search and when applying. What we have in common with families of other races are the timeline, policies, and procedures of the college admissions process. Some rules and requirements must be adhered to regardless of whether you are applying to PWIs or HBCUs. We explain the application process so that you and your child will understand what will be expected of you. This process must be intentionally managed and executed in order for your child to have college admissions success.

The college application process has many moving parts. Its foundational components may be similar to what they were twenty to thirty years ago, but the changes that the process has undergone and the strategies your child needs to employ to better their chances of being admitted should not be underestimated.

Overwhelmingly in our interviews and roundtable discussions with Black parents, most assumed the process started during or at the end of the eleventh grade, or even worse, some said senior year. This is not true. The process has to start much earlier than that. It must start with students choosing the right classes in the ninth grade. This lays the foundation for possible honors, advanced, Advanced Placement, or International Baccalaureate courses later in high school. In tenth grade, they'll be on a trajectory where they can start to consider selective universities based on the classes they're taking. During the ninth and tenth grades, they can also get involved in extracurricular activities and gradually become leaders. Around the same time, they can take diagnostic standardized tests to determine which test may be better for them. This is just a snapshot of the steps students should take early in their high school experience. It was hard for us to hear school counselor interviewees, Black and white, tell us that Black parents are too often "late to the game" or not engaged enough in the college preparation process. Those who are best prepared and armed with information early will win the game when it's time.

Throughout this book we have emphasized how the college admissions process is individualized and specific to every student and family, so we find it difficult to give definite answers to questions such as these:

1. When should a family begin the college search process?
2. How many colleges should a student apply to?
3. What are the chances of the student getting into a particular college?

Our answer most of the time is "it depends," especially when it comes to selective colleges and universities, both PWIs and HBCUs. We sometimes have a parent or counselor tell us what they heard about why a student was admitted or was not admitted to a school in an effort to draw a comparison with another student. In most instances, though, there are few similarities shared by any two applicants. So, our first bit of advice is to take information you hear from others about the college admissions process with a grain of salt, because there is no formula that guarantees admission.

We are not going to tell you what type of school your student should be looking at, but we do think it is important to provide some guidance that will help parents and students when they think about building a college list. Given the differences in our experiences, I (Tim) will come at the process from the "macro" view of a college admissions officer, and Shereem will examine it from a "micro" view given his experience working directly with students and families as a college counselor and consultant.

Once students get a sense of the schools they want to apply to, they may be interested in a school their family cannot afford. I am a big proponent of having that conversation early on in the process to manage expectations. In our experience, a lot of the anxiety can be mitigated with open communication about cost and what resources are available to fund the student's education.

Currently, many schools are touting being test-optional, but the reality is that standardized testing remains an important part of admissions for the foreseeable future. Near the end of their sophomore year, students should begin to think about testing and have a sense of how well they have tested in the past in order to decide whether they will need test prep going into their junior year. I would recommend that students take a diagnostic version of the SAT or ACT to find out how well they do; the results will help the family formulate a plan going into the student's senior year. Families may determine that it's best to apply only to test-optional schools, get some test prep to improve the student's scores, or change the schools the student will apply to based on their score. No matter what, we encourage all students to take the SAT or ACT at least once, particularly if they intend to apply for scholarships.

As students enter their senior year, that is the time to firm up their college list and identify scholarship opportunities. Students should narrow down their list to eight to twelve schools. Some families may choose to apply to more schools than that, but in our professional opinion, having more than fifteen schools demonstrates a student's lack of focus. In addition, without fee waivers or using the Common Black College Application, which has a one-time fee of twenty dollars to apply to participating schools, submitting college

applications can become expensive. Selective PWI college application fees frequently range from fifty to one hundred dollars. By no
means are we telling you how to spend your money, but we want
you to be smart about it given the cost of higher education and the
low admit rate at many selective institutions.

The next part of the process is connecting with schools and
asking questions specific to your college needs. At this time students
should have a good sense of what they want out of their college
experience. In the summer before their senior year and in the fall,
students should formally engage with college admissions advisors
and ask questions. Colleges and universities expect their admissions
officers to meet virtually with students online via Zoom, or prior to
the pandemic, officers used to travel around the country and the
world to connect with prospective applicants. I (Tim) always offer
my email and phone number as a resource to students whom I meet
and invite them to ask me further questions when they have them.
Sadly, too few students and families take advantage of the offer.
Admissions officers are your best informational resource for the admissions process, so please connect with them and take advantage
of the information they can share.

Tim and I (Shereem) chose to write this book together, not only
because we both have extensive admissions experience but also because we have different opinions. This makes for spirited discussions (occasionally arguments) that let us hear (hopefully) the other
person's points and decide whether to accept them. I do not share
Tim's view that the college search should start in the ninth grade. I
would say seventh grade, and I can even argue for third grade. That's
because I come from an independent school background, where
college awareness started before children could read. I read in an
article in *Los Angeles* magazine that the esteemed Buckley School
once had a sign at the school's entrance that read, "College begins
at two," a favorite saying of Isabelle Buckley, who founded the K–12
school in 1933. The school boasts 100 percent college acceptance
for its graduates.

The classes your child takes in middle school, especially in math, sciences, and foreign languages, affect the classes they will take in high school. This influences how rigorous their classes are and how selective universities will determine if they are prepared to handle the university's curriculum. Which classes your child takes matter a lot; this cannot be overstated. If your child wants to attend an elite PWI or HBCU, they must have a rigorous curriculum in high school, and they must do well in that rigorous curriculum.

The college admissions process begins with awareness in elementary school; setting an academic foundation begins in middle school; and an aspirational and action-oriented approach happens in high school. Over the years, your family should ask your child the questions below, and you should expect to hear evolving and gradually more mature responses.

- What is college?
- Why do people go?
- What happens there?
- What is the goal of going?

If we have conversations about these questions with our children in elementary school, they can begin to do their own research and then take appropriate courses and participate in extracurricular activities. College preparation is called a *process* for a reason. There are clear steps for students and parents to take that will make the process more manageable.

Timeline for Success: Grades Nine to Twelve

Please review this checklist with your child and adjust it as is appropriate for their aspirations and learning style.

Ninth Grade—Students
1. Get adjusted to high school academically and get the best grades possible.

2. Start exploring what extracurricular activities are offered (clubs, sports, community service, fine and performing arts).
3. Start to document activities, academic and extracurricular accomplishments, summer and work experiences.
4. Focus on time management skills: When will you do homework? How much time does it take you to complete homework thoroughly? What are you doing with your free time?
5. Discuss summer opportunities (e.g., a job or a summer course) with your school counselor and parents, and research them on your own.

Ninth Grade—Parents

- Have you discussed paying for college with your child? How much money have you saved? What is the budget?
- Questions to ask a school counselor:
  - Do ninth graders take the PSAT?
  - What is the sequence of courses to take that will lead to honors, advanced, or Advanced Placement (AP) courses later in high school?
  - How can my child take those classes and when?
  - When should my child visit or virtually connect with schools to demonstrate interest?

Tenth Grade—Students

1. Complete a personality or strength-finders assessment to learn more about your strengths, interests, and possible majors and careers. This will help with course selection.
2. Continue to explore extracurricular activities and start to think about possible leadership positions.
3. Update your documented activities and accomplishments list. This will become the basis for a resume.
4. Grades start to really matter, so you should be working hard and learning what subjects you like and excel in. You'll want

to take honors, advanced, and AP courses, if possible. Meet with your school counselor and a college admissions expert to discuss your plans.

5. Take the PSAT, if offered (in the fall).
6. Take a practice SAT and ACT (in the spring) to determine which one is better for you.
7. Be sure to use your summer productively and have a plan to work, volunteer, or do a project.
8. Start to research and build a list of colleges that you're interested in (see below).

Tenth Grade—Parents

- Schedule a local college visit or one while on vacation so that you can start to familiarize your child with different schools.
- Discuss possible majors and careers with your child using their personality and strength-finders assessment as the primary source of information.

How to Build a College List

There are four core factors to consider when creating a college list:

1. Cost
2. Location
3. Possible major
4. Possible career

Start with these and then add other factors that matter to your family. Parents need to be clear with students about how cost and location may bear on the choice of colleges. Students should have taken a personality, strength-finders, or career assessment to assist them in identifying possible majors and careers. Here are other factors to consider:

Size of school and size of academic departments that your child is interested in. Size affects how many courses are offered. Are professors accessible if a student needs additional help?

Academic reputation: Do college experts perceive this to be a "good school?" What is the ROI (return on investment)? (collegefactual.com) Does this college set students up for success after graduation?

How diverse is the student body racially, culturally, geographically, and socioeconomically?

What kinds of students are on campus? Percentages of Black students, white students, Latinx students, Asian and Pacific Islanders, Native and Indigenous, and international students?

What is the four-year graduation rate?

What is the average class size?

What are the housing and dining options?

How selective is the school (that is, hard to get into), and should you even apply if the school has a low acceptance rate?

How safe is the campus? What is the school's relationship with local law enforcement?

Are there fraternities and sororities? Is that important?

Are there religious services on campus? Are students required to attend?

What are the social and extracurricular activity opportunities on campus?

Do sports or Greek life dominate the social experience on weekends?

What is there to do off campus?

What kinds of job, career, or entrepreneurial preparation happens at the school?

Eleventh Grade—Students

This is the most important year of high school for college admissions preparation. Set clear academic goals and work hard. You are at the point when you must be aware of who you are and what's important to you and get excited about exploring all the possibilities that colleges offer.

Fall

1. Review your social media accounts and pay attention to what you post. *Nothing is private in social media*, and colleges may review the social media accounts of prospective students.
2. Review personality and strength-finders assessment, and take it again if necessary.
3. Start the year off strong; review your transcript and junior-year schedule. Are you taking honors, advanced, or AP courses?
4. Register for and take standardized tests (PSAT, ACT, or SAT).
5. Continue to invest yourself in extracurricular activities and seek out positions of leadership.
6. Start to visit colleges on school holidays, preferably when college students are on campus. (Ask a school counselor about getting excused absences for these visits.)
7. Pay close attention to twelfth graders and their college application process.
8. Prepare for fall college visits (by coming up with questions to ask, etc.).
9. Ask a school counselor if you can join in-school college information sessions.

Eleventh Grade—Parents

- Attend a financial aid and college scholarship workshop or webinar.
- Schedule college visits.

Winter
1. Start to investigate summer opportunities and apply for programs, jobs, and internships.
2. Continue to research colleges, build your list, and visit campuses.
3. Register for senior-year courses and consider how specific courses will influence your application. Are you taking honors, advanced, or AP courses? In subjects or majors you want to pursue in college?

Eleventh Grade—Parents

- Review your family calendars for opportunities to visit schools.
- Schedule a meeting with a school counselor and attend school-sponsored college admissions workshops.

Spring
1. Discuss your college list with your school counselor with reference to your present transcript, test scores, and activities.
2. Start filling out college applications. (Most schools will use the Common Application, Coalition Application, or Common Black College Application, but some schools will have their own application.)
3. Brainstorm in response to application essay prompts.
4. Ask teachers for college recommendation letters.
5. Become a leader in your extracurricular activity for the upcoming twelfth grade, revise your resume, and add *all* high school activities.
6. Take the ACT or SAT and decide how many more times, if any, you need to retake it.
7. Plan to visit colleges.
8. Confirm summer plans.
9. Confirm senior-year class schedule.
10. Attend college fair or college information sessions to connect with admissions officers.

11. Discuss possibly applying Early Decision or Early Action.
12. Start to demonstrate interest to top colleges on your list (opening emails, following their social media accounts, attending virtual information sessions, engaging with admissions offices).
13. Be sure to submit what your high school guidance counselor asks of you ahead of all deadlines.
14. Attend any essay and application workshops offered by your high school.

Eleventh Grade—Parents

Questions to ask a school counselor:

- Can my child meet with college admissions representatives in their junior year when the representatives visit in person or virtually in the fall?
- When should we start to visit campuses virtually on our own?
- When is the junior-year college information presentation?
- Do you have any sample case studies of applicants for us to review?
- Is there a list of graduates from this high school who would be willing to speak with us about their experience at institutions of interest to us?
- What information goes into the school counselor recommendation?
- Do you read the teacher recommendations before they are sent?
- Can we see the school profile that you send to colleges?
- How often will we be able to meet with you?

Summer (between Eleventh and Twelfth Grades)

1. Relax and rejuvenate.
2. Enjoy your resume-building summer courses and activities.
3. Refine your college list after reviewing your final grades from junior year.
4. Research the types of applications, requirements, and deadlines that colleges and universities have.

5. Begin to draft your personal and supplemental essays, if you have not already.
6. Continue to work on the Common Application.
7. Register for virtual information sessions and interviews.
8. Continue with standardized test prep, if necessary.
9. Visit more colleges.

Late Summer (August)

1. The Common Application "rolls over" and can be submitted as early as August 1.
2. Start the Coalition Application, if necessary.
3. Revise personal statement and supplemental essays.
4. Register for interviews, if applicable.
5. Ask summer employers or mentors for an additional recommendation, if applicable.
6. Continue with standardized test prep, if necessary.
7. Take standardized test, if applicable.

Twelfth Grade—Students

Early Fall (September)

1. Finalize college list.
2. Keep track of all deadlines, applications completed, and what you have submitted to colleges.
3. Attend college informational sessions in person or online.
4. Discuss Early Decision and Early Action strategies.
5. Revise personal statement and supplemental essays.
6. Register for interviews, if applicable.
7. Proofread all Early Action and Early Decision applications and essays.
8. Take standardized tests for the last time, if applicable.
9. Actively look for scholarships.
10. Follow up with all recommendation writers.
11. Be sure to submit all the documents your high school guidance counselor asks for.

Twelfth Grade—Parents

- Meet with a high school counselor to understand their timeline, expectations, and procedures.
- Review (but do not revise) your student's essay(s) and share feedback.
- Proofread all of your student's essays and applications.

Fall (October and November)

1. Complete and submit all Early Action or Early Decision applications.
2. Complete and submit applications for all schools requiring a portfolio.
3. Have Early Action and Early Decision interviews, if applicable.
4. Ask a school counselor if and when your first quarter grades are being sent to your Early Action / Early Decision schools, if applicable.
5. Finalize a list of those schools where you'll apply by the regular decision deadline and complete applications and essays.
6. Review application(s) submission and interview deadlines for regular decision.
7. Begin to apply for scholarships.

Twelfth Grade—Parents
Confirm that all financial aid information has been submitted.

Winter (December and January)

1. Discuss Early Decision II strategies, if applicable.
2. Regular decision and Early Decision II applications are generally due on or around January 1. Submit them in mid-December so that everyone can have a relaxing holiday break.

Winter (January–March)

1. If your Early Decision application is deferred by a college that you want to attend, correspond with the college and indicate that it is still a top choice. Offer any updates on activities, awards, and accomplishments.
2. Learn more about financing a college education over four years by attending workshops.
3. Beware of senioritis! This is when seniors get too comfortable and do not finish their senior year strong. This can lead to admission offers being rescinded or to being put on academic probation as a freshman in college.
4. Wait for application decisions.

Spring (March and April)

1. Receive decisions from schools and evaluate admission and financial aid options.
2. Visit colleges that you've been accepted to and are considering.
3. If waitlisted, consider remaining on the list and communicating with the school that you will attend, if this is in fact true.
4. Attend accepted students' receptions when possible.
5. Make a final decision and submit a deposit by May 1.

Spring (May)

1. Celebrate College Signing Day! Wear a shirt with your new school's name on it.
2. Notify your school counselor and any scholarships of your final decision.
3. Have your final transcript sent.
4. Sign up for campus housing.
5. Join freshmen social media groups to find a roommate.

Postsecondary School: The Transfer Option

Having the opportunity to revise our book for a second edition, we wanted to add a discussion on transferring from one institution of higher education to another.

Life is not linear, and sometimes college isn't either. Transferring colleges is more common than ever for students following the COVID-19 pandemic, an unstable economy, and the popularity of "pivoting." Students may not have entered college with the intent to transfer; however, the reality is that thousands of students transfer every year for any number of reasons. Sometimes the reasons are personal and unrelated to their current institution, but other times students transfer because the place where they enrolled did not live up to their expectations.

Many people who enroll in a junior or community college after high school transfer from there to a four-year institution. They may earn an associate's degree (after two years of study) from a junior college and then attend a four-year institution to earn a bachelor's degree (after four years of study). We have not discussed community/junior colleges, but they make up a significant part of higher education in the United States. According to the National Student Clearinghouse Research Center, 30 percent of US undergraduates are enrolled at public two-year colleges; these schools offer benefits like open-enrollment policies and flexible scheduling for working students. Community colleges may also serve as the first college experience for dual-enrollment students in high school who decide to take a college-level course before going to college. There are many famous Black people who started at, attended, or graduated from community colleges: Gabrielle Union, Halle Berry, Morgan Freeman, and Queen Latifah, to name but a few.

Transferring from one school to another is the prerogative of a student, but transferring also benefits institutions as a tool for managing their student enrollment. All four-year colleges experience attrition, which is what happens when students withdraw or take a leave of absence; a college generally moves to fill the vacated spots in order to maintain its target number for enrollment. Having as many matriculated (that is, enrolled) students as fits its plan is what colleges want for two reasons: (a) more tuition money comes in, and (b) more young people get a chance to receive a higher education. In 2022 Princeton University announced that it plans to increase the number of transfer students it will accept in upcoming years to boost its enrollment of undergraduates from first-generation, lower-income, military, or community-college backgrounds.

After a student has attended a college or university for a semester or year, the student and their family can assess how the experience at the institution is going. Parents can ask their student questions like these:

Are you doing well academically?

Are you having fun?

Are you taking full advantage of opportunities there?
(Or are you wasting my money?!)

Students can ask themselves questions like these:

Do I belong here?

Do I have friends here?

Is this school going to help me get to the next level in life?

Transferring to another school is a big decision to make and so must be thought through carefully. Understanding whether and how course credits earned will transfer across institutions, and if transferring will delay a student's graduation because credits do not, is a concern that should figure in that decision.

How Transferring Works

To transfer colleges, students can follow these general steps:

1. *Research and explore.* Look into different colleges or universities you are interested in transferring to. Consider factors such as cost, location, major, and career.

2. *Check transfer requirements.* There's a good chance that students will lose some credits earned from their first institution if they choose to transfer. Review the transfer admission requirements of the colleges you are considering. These requirements may include minimum GPA, prerequisite coursework, and standardized test scores.

3. *Contact the admissions office.* Reach out to the admissions office of the colleges you are interested in transferring to. They can provide details about the transfer process, application deadlines, and any additional requirements.

4. *Request transcripts.* Request that your current institution send your official college transcript to the schools you are applying to as a transfer student. These transcripts should include your course taken, grades earned, and any transferable credits.

5. *Meet with an advisor.* Schedule a meeting with an academic advisor at your current college to discuss your plan to transfer. The advisor can provide guidance on course selection and ensure you are on track to meet transfer requirements.

6. *Prepare application materials.* Complete the transfer applications for your chosen colleges. These applications typically require personal essays, letters of recommendation, and other supporting documents. Be sure to submit all required materials before the application deadline.

7. *Financial aid considerations.* If you are currently receiving financial aid, contact the financial aid offices at both your current institution and the colleges you are applying to. They can advise you on transferring financial aid and on scholarship opportunities.

Any parent reading this book knows that life is not about where you start but rather how you finish. In our opinion, transferring should be celebrated when students who are maturing in their college years learn of alternatives they didn't know about when applying to college the first time around. Sometimes, though, a student's drive to transfer has nothing to do with dissatisfaction over their current institution; rather, they desire to attend what they or their parents perceive to be a better institution. "Trading up" is a notion that many students and their families entertain when they continue to aspire to a better-known or more prestigious school than the one they entered out of high school. We don't recommend letting the desire to trade up dictate your decision-making, but we acknowledge that it happens frequently.

If you are looking to transfer, here are some trade-offs we want to bring to your attention:

- More than likely you will lose some course credits you have already earned. Review the websites of schools you are considering to determine how many of your current credits they will accept. You may have taken courses at your current school that will not count at your new college or university.
- There is little to no merit-based financial aid available to transfer students in comparison with those applying to enter as first-year enrollees. Need-based aid will be available at the schools you're considering, but any scholarship or merit money you have currently will likely not follow you to your new institution. You'll have to weigh the financial consequences of transferring.
- Depending on when you plan on transferring, there may not be guaranteed housing at the new institution. Living on campus is a significant part of the college experience for some students. If that is true for you, know that there may be limited options for on-campus lodging available to transfer students.
- Orientation programs for transfer students vary from school to school, and few of them are as immersive or as welcoming as an orientation for arriving first-year students. If integrating in the campus community ranks high in your priorities for your new school, you should look into how your potential schools assimilate transfer students.

The transfer process will vary depending on the colleges and universities you are applying to, so you must check the transfer policies and requirements of each institution and communicate with the admissions offices at those institutions.

CHAPTER 15

What Are Colleges Looking For?

Overview

Each college has different admissions requirements and selection criteria, but the principles we describe in this chapter are consistent with selective college admissions. If you follow them, we are confident that your child will be successful in the college search and application processes.

———

Every college your child applies to will want to see the three-to-four-year track record of the classes they took and the grades they got in them. In other words, **the most important part of your child's application is their transcript.** Colleges are looking for students who have shown that they want to learn and were engaged over four years and challenged themselves with an array of courses. For your child to be considered by a selective university, HBCU or PWI, **they must have taken a rigorous high school curriculum that includes honors, Advanced Placement, dual enrollment, or International Baccalaureate courses, if possible.** For those who attended a school that offers these courses and chose not to take them, they're putting themselves at a disadvantage.

Getting high grades in hard courses helps students get into selective schools. GPAs and class rank matter for most colleges in their admissions. Colleges want applicants to show they are eager and capable students who got good grades in high school. Yet, in some instances, receiving slightly lower grades in a rigorous curriculum is preferable to receiving all As in less challenging classes.

Please note, though, that there are degrees of selectivity. Some colleges, PWIs and HBCUs, will not accept students with a B average, which is roughly a 3.0 GPA. There are exceptions, of course, but they are rare among the most selective schools in the country. Each college publishes GPA averages for admission. The expectations are not written in stone, but you and your child should be aware of them, and your child's GPA should fall within the published range. All colleges have institutional priorities for what sorts of students they want to or need to admit each year. What does that mean? It means that college admissions offices are in the business of admitting a class, not necessarily a student. They take students who will make the class diverse and whole.

The Role of the College or School Counselor

The role of the school or college counselor is to support, guide, and serve as a partner with the family through the college search and application processes. Overwhelmingly, school counselors are influential and encouraging advocates for students and their aspirations. However, there are some who do not properly research and gauge the college landscape for how it affects Black students. In her memoir *Becoming*, Michelle Obama reflects on an unfortunate encounter she had with her school counselor in high school. In her senior year she met with the counselor she had been assigned and was disappointed when the counselor said, "I'm not sure . . . that you're Princeton material." Imagine how damaging this educational professional's swift and dismissive judgment was for a young Michelle. She stated that she blocked out this memory for a long time and admittedly could not recall the age, race, or any physical characteristics of the counselor. The counselor underestimated the future First Lady. Michelle Obama did wind up attending Princeton University and went on to get a law degree from Harvard Law School. Her experience, however, is not uncommon.

Justice Ketanji Brown Jackson, the first Black woman appointed to the US Supreme Court, also has said she had an unsupportive school counselor, who told her that she'd never get into Harvard. She proved that counselor wrong. We mention these accomplished Black women with the hope that your Black child does not have to disprove the same doubt.

This is a classic case of what we call undermatching. Undermatching happens when a school counselor does not believe in the potential of a student to be a competitive applicant and so may discourage the student and their family from applying to selective schools. Ideally, the family and college counselor should work together to determine what type of school and environment is best for the student. In doing this, both the family and the counselor must be open and honest about the student's preparation, maturity, and, yes, the family's finances. This relationship between family and counselor should begin as early as the ninth grade and be nurtured over the course of four years. For the student to have college admissions success—that is, to have choices in where they go to college—the family and the school counselor have to be transparent about abilities, expectations, and ambitions. The adults have to communicate in order to achieve this goal.

The high school counselors we interviewed in our research worked in public or independent schools. Here are the questions we asked them:

1. How did you get into the college counseling profession?
2. What has been your experience counseling Black students and families?
3. Generally speaking, do Black families come to you with the same amount of college information as families of other races?
4. What do you wish more Black parents knew about college counseling?
5. Do you recommend HBCUs to Black families, and how do they react to the recommendation? What schools—HBCUs or PWIs—are most popular and why?

The responses to questions 1 and 2 varied, and question 5 required some discussion. We were alarmed, though, by the consistent responses we got to questions 3 and 4. We heard that Black families too often gather information about colleges in the spring of their child's eleventh grade or, even worse, in the fall of their twelfth grade. This late timing contrasts with other families, who often visit colleges, encourage extracurricular activities, and explore options for standardized test preparation earlier in their child's high school career. Some may want to attribute this difference to resources, but we disagree. We think it's much more about Black parents being too comfortable with what we know and about not acknowledging how college admissions has changed.

One of the biggest challenges in the college admissions process is that too many people want a voice in what the student should do. Yes, advice from friends and family is well intentioned, yet it is often misinformed. Many people who give advice about college admissions are not professionals in the field. Although they may have gone through the college admissions process with their own child, they should not substitute for a school counselor. A school counselor is supposed to be an authority on the process and can help your student build a balanced college list. The counselor should not be avoided and often is the only person that colleges and universities will share information with about a student's application; thus you are better off engaging with the counselor early on to decide if the information they are sharing—rooted in data and statistics—is applicable to you. Independent college advisors may be able to offer alternative perspectives on college lists and make suggestions for essays and application strategies. In a case where your family hires an independent college advisor, you should let your child's school know about it for the purpose of transparency and clear communication.

We know that some of you may be cautious about school counselors and wonder how they work with Black students after hearing a story like Michelle Obama's. We have similar concerns and will address them below. However, we thought it would be valuable for you to know what school counselors think about themselves, their roles, and your Black children. Here are themes that arose in our conversations with public and private school counselors. These are direct quotations.

On college admissions today . . .

"The criteria to get into college [have] changed a lot in the past fifteen to twenty years since many parents graduated, yet many of them come to the process with assumptions about the process that are often dated and not based in fact. This leads to setting unrealistic expectations, which does not help to set the foundation of the college search process."

On the cost of higher education . . .

"Many families don't have open conversations with their children about the finances. Thus, when students are developing their college list, they have no concept of what the family can and cannot afford when it comes time to make a college choice."

On the importance of starting early . . .

"Depending on the type of college the student is looking to apply to, beginning the process junior and senior year is far too late given some of the curriculum requirements. Most counselors think the process should start at the latest in the ninth grade."

On understanding there are multiple pathways to success . . .

"Some parents come to this process thinking that the only majors that students can be successful in are biology, business, engineering, or a couple of other areas, when the reality is many colleges and universities have [lots of] majors. In addition to that, most of the jobs that are being created are not in many of those areas and have yet to be created."

On the college visit . . .

"Most college counselors feel very strongly [opposed to] students committing to a college . . . they have never visited. Thus, visiting colleges, in person or virtually, if possible, is a very important part of the process."

Parents should always ask their school counselor if they are involved with NACAC (National Association of College Admission Counseling). This is an international professional organization composed of college admissions and high school counselors who work hand-in-hand to guide students from secondary to postsecondary education. All college admissions and college counseling professionals are welcome to join the organization, which provides opportunities for professional development, continuing education, and networking. Given that it costs to be a member and to attend many of the organization's events, NACAC has several initiatives aimed at getting more high school counselors involved in the organization.

Most independent schools have an office dedicated to college counseling with staff members whose sole purpose is to help students with the college admissions process. This office operates independently of the school's counseling office, which handles students' mental health and other counseling needs. Depending on the size of the school, caseloads for counselors could be anywhere between thirty and fifty students per grade. By contrast, many public school counselors have responsibilities beyond college counseling and have caseloads numbering from two hundred to four hundred students or more. One veteran college counselor we interviewed, who had worked at both a large public school and an independent school, had this to say:

"When I was at my independent school, we had thirty juniors and thirty seniors that were in my caseload. When we transitioned to public school, we had a caseload of five hundred students between

the junior and senior classes, where there was no real college-going culture. In addition to the bigger caseloads, there is a belief that the work of counselors does not extend beyond the building; thus your focus should be on the work that needs to happen in the high school and not relationship building with colleges and universities, a luxury we had when I was in the independent school."

Most counselors have a bachelor's degree at a minimum, but many have a master's degree in some form of counseling or in education. There is no such thing, however, as a "college counseling bachelor's degree." While there is a growing number of graduate programs with a college counseling focus, most of them emphasize the guidance and counseling aspect of the job and give little attention to the scope of colleges and universities in the country and around the world. The reality is that most high school and college counselors have to educate themselves about the many colleges and universities available to students.

There are more than four thousand colleges and universities in the United States. It is unrealistic to expect that anyone would know about all of them, but we hope that counselors have a good sense of the different school types that are available. These range from two-year colleges, HBCUs, state schools, and private schools. The guidance that counselors give depends on their knowledge of schools, and if that knowledge is limited, so too will be the suggestions they make to students. In our interviews with school counselors, both Black and white, almost all admitted to having extremely limited understanding of HBCUs beyond the Black Ivies, and those who did understand more tended to be from the South.

This knowledge base is important for Black families who have questions about more than admissions chances, academic majors, and location. They may have questions about resources specific to Black students, the percentage of Black students on campus, graduation and retention rates, and campus climate—questions that may not be as important for their non-Black counterparts. You may have a lot of trust in the college counseling office, but know that you should communicate your child's needs up front to your counselor.

Building a College List

As a college counselor for the past twenty years, I (Shereem) have talked to many students and parents about "match" and "fit." I often urge students to consider who they are, what they want to do, and whether and how a school will help them get there. Students need to understand the importance of finding a school that is right for them, one where they will excel academically and socially and have a college community that suits their personality. Given all the colleges and universities in the United States, I am confident that many schools will match what a student wants. Students or parents who believe that one particular school is the only place where the student will be happy wind up limiting themselves. Researching and visiting colleges can be incredibly fun. Learning about academic programs and extracurricular offerings at colleges can help students find their niche and, ultimately, a career.

One caution: college rankings can serve a valuable purpose, but no one should ever rely on one source to determine what schools are good or not so good. We believe that rankings—*U.S. News and World Report, Forbes, Princeton Review*—generate interest in schools. They are points of comparison regarding resources, reputation, and facilities. However, there are other factors that students should consider in their decision-making. They need to think about what's important to them—majors, activities, the types of students they want to be with—and how they will make the most of their college years.

My (Shereem's) company offers a service called the College List Builder, which, in essence, is me and my team building a college list for a student. Once we have gathered information from parents and the student, we're able to suggest twenty-plus colleges, given what we know from having visited more than five hundred colleges and universities over the years and from some expensive, exclusive tools that we use. These are not simple algorithms available from free websites; we conduct a data-rich analysis that we use to confirm or reject initial ideas. We love building lists for families and opening their eyes to schools they may have never heard of or strategies for admission they may have never considered. We build college lists based on four primary factors: *cost, location, possible major*, and *possible career*. Each factor has a distinct importance to the college search process.

Cost

College is very, very expensive. Many of us, including me, are first-generation college students whose parents were blue-collar workers. Having families with limited income and assets, many of us were awarded financial aid packages that were loan-heavy. We know not to let our children take on an exorbitant amount of loan debt. Moreover, if we now have a higher income than our parents had, our children will not qualify for as much financial aid as we did. You and your child must therefore decide how much you are willing to spend or can afford. We are not in favor of taking out excessive college loans. In the chapter "Show Me the Money," we explained some basic elements of financing college and described what you can do to tackle the cost of college.

Location

Where a school is located is something to consider. Is the school in an urban, suburban, or rural setting? What is the weather there like? Many of the most selective schools, as deemed by *U.S. News and World Report*, are in the Northeast, but students who are not from that part of the country should take weather into consideration. Additionally, given that a student will spend four years at a school, they should look into the social and cultural outlets available off campus. Can they mature as a young adult in this environment? Can they get a part-time job off campus if desired? What internship opportunities are available locally? Do the internships often lead to full-time job offers?

Possible Major

Students' primary goal in going to college should be to immerse themselves in an academic field of study that suits their strengths and interests. Their major should be a "practical" one that leads to a career that is both fulfilling and worthy of the financial investment of going to college. Students should have a major in mind when they apply to college. Their choice of major may change, of course, and a liberal arts school encourages students to explore their intellectual interests. Being "undecided" when enrolling in college, however, is often a recipe for wasting time and money. We go into depth about this in chapter 5, "What Is a Liberal Arts Education, and Is It Worth It?" There are personality and career assessment tools that can introduce students to possible majors as early as the tenth grade. Please note, though, we are not advocating that students declare a major in pre-med, engineering, computer science, or business if they do not have the ambition, high school courses, interest, or strengths to excel in one of these fields. Majors do not equal a career; they just put students on a *possible* (operative word) career path.

Possible Career

We do not know any Black parents who want their child to go to college and come out unemployed or without a plan for having a fulfilling and remunerative career. We want our children to be financially independent and expect college to be the first step toward accomplishing this. A possible major and a possible career go hand-in-hand when building a college list. Having a vision for your child's professional life is not "controlling" them. It's helping them explore options that you know are possible and they may not be aware of. Our duty as parents is to steer our children to their strengths and lead them to majors and careers.

Investigating a college's career guidance office is a must:

- What kinds of career advising happen there?
- What companies does the school have a relationship with?

- How strong is the alumni network?
- What do most alumni do for work soon after graduation, and how much do they earn?

The answer to some of these questions, especially about income after graduation, can be found at the College Scorecard website of the US Department of Education (collegescorecard.ed.gov).

Visiting Colleges: How, Why, and When

Prior to the COVID-19 pandemic, any college admissions officer or college counselor would likely have told you that the best way to find out if a college is right for your child is to visit its campus. With the arrival of the pandemic, however, higher education had to suspend or limit in-person tours, information sessions, and campus programming in favor of giving students and families a virtual semblance of visiting campus. Institutions launched all kinds of virtual platforms to connect with students; the reality, though, is that there is no substitute for visiting a campus in person.

Being able to walk around a campus, drop in at the dining hall, and imagine having a perfect day hanging out on campus helps students find a sense of place at a school. This is something we have witnessed many times: a student visits a campus recommended to them, with no expectations to like it, and by the end of the visit, something has happened that changes the student's mind. The thing is that you never really know what that something will be. It could be a connection with a tour guide, a sunny day on the quadrangle, or a great meal in the dining hall. More often than not, though, it's a general feeling not connected to any one thing about the experience. This feeling usually happens during or shortly after a college visit.

When you begin your college exploration, ideally in your sophomore and junior years of high school, here are our suggestions for how to get a good feel for a school when you visit its campus:

Attend a virtual or in-person (based on availability) information session and go on a tour. While information sessions can sometimes be a bit boring, they are a good way of learning what a school prioritizes. Use this opportunity to learn what the school presents, values, and emphasizes. This will give you insight into what your experience would be like were you to enroll there. Pay attention to the questions asked by other prospective students as well as their cultural and racial backgrounds.

Ask questions. Make sure to ask questions that are important to you and your college exploration process. We suggest having questions prepared prior to attending the information session. Being on campus is your time to find out the things you want to know. Don't leave campus with unanswered questions. There is no question about the academic programs, application review process, or campus culture that you should not be able to get an answer to. Why visit a campus if you are not going to get all the information you need to have an informed opinion about it? (Parents should do the same.)

Speak to a student whom you identify with or share an interest with. You don't have to speak with a Black student, but we do recommend that you speak with someone who has a similar academic interest, is from your hometown, or has another connection with you that matters. While your experience of the school will not be the same as theirs, they can provide you with insight into the campus culture and student experience.

Eat a meal on campus. This is important to do. You should know what dining options are available at the school. No matter how good the food is, you will grow tired of it if you eat it often enough. However, if you don't like the food or the school doesn't have the dietary options you desire, you will know the school's limitations.

Explore on your own. You may not see all that you were wanting to see while on the campus tour. We would advise you to build in some time just to walk around campus and explore areas that you may be interested in. We know that students and families sometimes have the best experiences and conversations on a campus outside the formal tour.

When to Visit

If you want to get the most out of your visit, and we know that you do, you should visit when classes are in session. That is when you can see what the campus "looks" and "feels" like when all the students, faculty, and staff are there. There will be more people around for you to engage with. You will not be limited to what the admissions office or visitor center has to offer. When classes are in session, all the dining halls and student support offices will be open to your exploration.

The ideal time periods for a campus visit are after Labor Day through early November and from late January through April. Depending on the school, there may be limited opportunities to visit in April, given the occurrence of "yield" events related to admitted student programming. Visiting campuses during the summer may be convenient but is not ideal on account of the limited number of students on campus. A few campuses are lively year-round, but they are exceptions to the norm. We know that the months we recommend for visiting campuses are times when high school classes are also in session, but many high schools offer students some excused absences in their senior year for the purpose of visiting colleges.

Demonstrating Interest Can Help Your Child Get into College

In addition to visiting colleges, we are big advocates of demonstrating interest appropriately. Demonstrating interest is when a prospective student makes documented contact or connections with an institution. Some admissions offices will take this effort into consideration once a student applies for admission. Be sure to ask the schools you are interested in if they track demonstrated interest. Colleges love to be loved. They crave attention from the *right* students at the *right* time. Demonstrating interest to your top-choice schools can be critical to admission. Schools want to know that if they admit a student, there is a good likelihood that the student will enroll. We do not recommend, however, being too aggressive in demonstrating one's interest (assertive = good; aggressive = bad). Here are a few things high school students can do to engage with colleges.

"Like" a school's social media accounts. This is not as trivial as you might think. Colleges track their social media accounts just like most people and businesses do. If a student does not take the time to pop up on a list, do they really want to go there? Like a school on Facebook and follow it on Twitter and Instagram. Make sure to mention your top-choice schools in your own posts and tweets. And say nice things.

Have an interview. If a school offers interviews, then get some quality face time with a student ambassador, alumni interviewer, or an admissions officer. Many private colleges (and some public ones) offer prospective students the opportunity for an interview before they apply or afterward. These interviews help a student learn more about the college and help the college learn more about the student. Check the admissions office's website for this opportunity.

Write amazing supplemental essays. Nothing screams "I love you; please take me!" louder than knockout school-specific supplemental essays. In them, students can explain why they are a perfect fit for a school. In their applications, many colleges will ask directly, "Why do you want to come here?" Others will ask questions that reference their school's mission or strengths. The purpose of these essays is to gauge how much the student knows about the school and how well they will fit in at the school. Be sure to use your own voice and not just regurgitate what's on the school's website. Admissions officers like me (Tim) see right through this, so it is important to be original. Doing research about the school and demonstrating personal pizazz are key to good supplemental essays.

Early Decision and Early Action are *huge* **indicators of sincere interest**. Applying Early Decision is the strongest way to show a college that it is your number-one choice. This is why most colleges accept Early Decision applicants at a much higher rate than regular decision applicants. Early Decision is not for everyone, though, so if you aren't ready to commit to one school early in the game, apply Early Action instead, which still shows a high level of interest. It is important to submit applications before the deluge of other applicants submit theirs.

College Events to Attend

There are times of the school year when you can get a better feel for a campus than others; likewise there are events you can attend that can create a special connection and experience. While these experiences can provide you a glimpse into what your college experience could be, they will not reflect the totality of the college experience you will have. These events include going to a college rivalry game, such as Duke versus the University of North Carolina in college basketball, or being in the stands for the Bayou Classic football game in New Orleans between Grambling State University and Southern University.

Southern University and A&M College (HBCU)
Baton Rouge, LA
6,200 Undergraduates
Public
Graduate Students: Yes
Setting: Midsize City

These events can truly be exciting, and, yes, they are a part of the college experience for many. But think about the college experience outside these special events. What will your experience be like then? We are not trying to deter anyone from enjoying such events; rather, we are encouraging students and families to think about the daily experience that students will have at that institution. Many who attend college will have memories of going to the "big game," but more than that, they will remember the friends they met in the residence hall, the professor who pushed them in class, and the lessons they learned that stuck with them after graduation.

HBCU Homecomings

If you visit an HBCU on an ordinary day, you may not be as impressed with the campus grounds as you would be at a well-endowed PWI. To truly get a feel for these schools and what they can offer you in your college experience, we suggest that you visit on homecoming weekend. At homecoming, the campus really comes alive, and you can see what the school can provide students in identity and culture apart from what the school may seem to lack in resources. Homecoming at an HBCU is the epitome of the Black college experience. You will experience the essence of the school—its students, alumni, and rich history and culture. An HBCU homecoming is one of the greatest testaments to Black love, Black education, and Black accomplishment, and we encourage all to take part in one at least once.

Admissions Tests: ACT or SAT?

Standardized testing and standardized test preparation are both complicated. They are lucrative businesses and have become fixtures in college admissions. Many of the more selective schools in the United States require testing in some form for admissions. Testing has its benefits. It also has its drawbacks. The merits of standardized testing have been debated for decades, but COVID-19 disrupted higher education in ways that have pushed this debate further. While there was a growing number of schools that had test-optional admissions before the pandemic of 2020 and 2021, it pushed schools to offer test-optional admissions on account of the uncertainty about public health safety at testing sites. According to FairTest.org, in 2021 over 75 percent of US colleges and universities offering bachelor's degrees were either test-optional or test-blind, an all-time high. We think this is a trend that will continue for the foreseeable future, but many of these schools have not made a long-term commitment to being test-optional beyond the next few years. In addition to many institutions going test-optional, the NCAA will not require students to take a standardized test to meet the NCAA's initial eligibility requirements for Division I or II athletics through the 2022–23 academic year. Despite these suspended requirements, testing is still part of the fabric of college admissions.

Beginning in March 2024, the SAT will be administered in a digital format only. There will no longer be an option to take the test on paper, unless a student qualifies for an exception. In addition to going digital, the test is shrinking to about two hours in duration. The College Board presents these as "student-friendly changes," with Priscilla Rodriguez, vice president of college-readiness assessments at the College Board, saying, "The digital SAT will be easier to take, easier to give, and more relevant." So far, reactions from students who sat for pilot administrations of the digital test have been positive.

What exactly has changed about the test? The new version of the SAT differs in noteworthy ways:

- The test lasts for about two hours, shrinking by one hour.
- There are two sections—a Reading & Writing section and a Math section—instead of four.
- Reading passages are shorter, and students answer only one question per passage.
- Students have more time per question.
- Students no longer receive separate Reading & Writing subscores.
- Students take the test on a laptop or tablet.

Test takers will need to download a digital testing app before test day. The app saves students' progress while they work, even if they lose internet access or their computer crashes. During pilot tests, a small number of students lost power, but all were ultimately able to submit their tests. Students will have access to a series of tools through the app, including a timer, an annotator, a calculator, a reference sheet, and a flagging tool to mark questions for review. The test is supposed to be adaptive. Each section begins with an introductory module. A student's performance on that first set of questions determines the difficulty level of the questions they'll see in the second module.

What's staying the same? Some aspects of the SAT are remaining as they were:

- Students will take the test at a school or test center, *not* at home.
- Scores are still out of 1600. Each section, Reading & Writing and Math, is scored on an 800-point scale. The College Board's extensive internal testing has shown that scores made on the paper and digital SAT are comparable. In fact, the College Board is encouraging universities to superscore across test formats. For that reason, the College Board and ACT do not have plans to update their concordance table, since scores will continue to align the way they do now. (Although there is active discussion about the ACT going digital, an official announcement has not been made at the time we write this.)
- Both sections feature multiple-choice questions. The Math section also includes questions that students must answer by entering their solutions directly into the app.
- Accommodations are available to students who need them. This includes taking the test on paper for those who qualify.

The pandemic forced many colleges and universities to adopt test-optional admission policies. More than 1,800 schools do not require the submission of standardized test scores at present, according to nonprofit FairTest, an organization that questions the use of standardized tests in admissions. The switch to a digital format,

FairTest said, "does not magically transform [the test] to a more accurate, fairer or valid tool for assessing college readiness."

We encourage families to examine how standardized tests are used and how to make testing benefit their student in the admissions process. We encourage all Black parents to consider investing in standardized test prep for their child because test scores are valuable information for many institutions. When your child scores well on the ACT or SAT, your child will be viewed as more competitive, and a good score may increase their chances of qualifying for scholarship money.

Standardized test scores are numbers that most admissions offices have depended on in evaluating applicants for a long time. Grades can be inflated, and curricula vary from high school to high school. Some schools have International Baccalaureate programs and others have Advanced Placement courses. Some schools have neither, so it's hard for colleges' admissions offices to evaluate students who had different course offerings or grading systems. The SAT and ACT, on the other hand, are common denominators that can give colleges a basis for comparing one student with another. Traditionally, these tests are viewed as measuring "aptitude." That may be a flawed way of thinking about them, but that's how admissions offices at some schools operate. When students are asked by friends or family about college, they are often asked "What are your test scores?" and "What is your GPA?" Seldom are they asked about their activities, recommendations, essays, or interviews.

Having a higher score on a test will open more doors. We also understand, however, that there are good test takers and those who don't test well. How well a student performs on standardized tests should determine if test-optional admission is the better choice.

Although taking standardized tests and buying stocks on the market are different things, I (Tim) found an analogy between them in a stock tip related to me by a friend. This friend, who works for an investment bank, was suggesting some possible stocks to invest in amid the pandemic. As he shared with me several options, some of them being tech plays, others being higher risk in the retail market, he ended by saying, "you can't go wrong with oil." He explained that while oil was currently down owing to low demand, there will continue to be a need for oil in future generations, even with our increased exploration and use of alternative energy sources. He concluded that oil will probably be around at least through our grandchildren's lives.

In the world of college admissions, testing is oil; it is not going anywhere anytime soon. Yes, some schools have become test-optional, and the pandemic increased the number of schools offering that option, but many of those schools may offer test-optional admissions only until things get back to normal. Then they will reinstate the requirement of testing in their admissions review.

Students may wonder if they should take the tests and submit scores with their applications. Akil Bello, an acclaimed educational policy advocate and testing expert, offers the following advice:

1. If you do not prep, do not test.
2. Start the process now and make decisions later (that is, prep first, take the test, and then decide whether to submit scores).
3. If you choose to take the test, say you're going prep "like it's 1999."

The truth is that you should do what is best for your student based on the schools they are looking to apply to. With so many variables in the college application process, no one factor is determinant, but testing is near the top of the list.

We think that many of those who are reading this book understand the *why* of applying to college, but just as important is the *how*. In this chapter we gave an overview of important parts in the admissions process to help ensure student success. As we were writing, we came across an article that quantified the information disparity that exists between Black families and white families when it comes to assisting students with the college admissions process. Susan Adams, in a December 2021 article in *Forbes* titled "White Students Have an Advantage in College Admissions," reported the results of a survey in which more than two-thirds of white students said they relied on family and friends to help them with college admissions, whereas only 38 percent of Black students got similar advice from their families. It is our goal through this book to close this gap so that Black families are better able to assist their children through the process of college admissions.

Acknowledgments

Tim

To my SpelHouse family: there are too many of you to name. But for all of those who allowed me to pick your brains, shared your family experiences to help me craft this book, have been down with me over the past twenty-five years, and continue to inspire me with all the great things you do, know that it means the world to me. Attending college in the Atlanta University Center is one of the best decisions I made in life and continues to be a great source of inspiration because of all of you. Rob, thanks for the inspiration years ago!

This book would never have been possible without the support of Emory University. Over my past twenty years, this great institution has allowed me to find my passion in an environment that aspires to be more than simply a place to go to college; rather, it aspires to be a destination where students transform their lives through sharing knowledge and creating community. All the wonderful, talented, and inspiring colleagues I have had the honor of working with, please know that each of you has made an impact on me and that this work would not have been possible without your reassurance. I often say that I have not worked a day since I arrived, and that is all because of you. To John Latting and Scott Allen, thank you for letting me be me; there is no way this book could exist without your support and encouragement.

To my Gates Millennium Scholars, UNCF, National Merit, QuestBridge, TRiO, College Horizons, the Black College Admissions Avengers (you know who you are!), and TDI families, along with all of the great admissions professionals and community-based organizations I have had the opportunity to work with from both sides of the desk—I can't thank you enough for being such a great source of inspiration and for the knowledge you have shared on top of all the great things you do to impact the lives of students looking to access higher education and beyond.

Shereem, thank you for picking up the phone to call me and then believing enough in me to let me take this journey with you. You may not have wanted me to answer your call, but I did, and your passion for this topic remains the catalyst for this important conversation. To my mother, father, sister, and brother, not a day goes by that I am not thankful for your presence in my life. Each of you has believed in me from day one, and I love you so much for it. This does not happen without the trips down I-20 from Dallas to Waskom and the foundation you all continue to provide me. And to all my day 1's from Texas, you "already" know!

Finally, Master Alexander, Miss Carter, Skinny, TT, and my rock Britney—thank you for the daily hugs, laughs, and inspiration. None of this happens without all the support you have given me throughout this process as I was locked in my lair writing.

Shereem

The historian Herman Dreer was a teacher, writer, author, and lecturer. I need to acknowledge how his writing on the brotherhood of Negro college men inspires me to do my best to be all that he was.

This book is a product of Tim's and my commitment to service. It's important that we start there. Everyone else who contributed to this book in some capacity did so because they too wanted to serve others. We appreciate the time and effort of all the people we spoke to about this project because you gave us insight and fuel.

To Greg Britton—thank you and your team at Johns Hopkins University Press for being excited and supportive from the beginning. You believe in us and we appreciate it.

To Brennan Barnard, Rick Clark, and Jeff Selingo—you guys set the table for us and shared your resources. Thank you.

To Cathleen Trigg-Jones and Dr. Tony Allen, president of Delaware State University—more than you know, you inspired our work and confirmed that it was important and necessary.

To some of the best people I know from Brooklyn Friends, Westtown, Wesleyan, Bread Loaf, and work life: André Wright, Ross

Stafford, Shawn Marshall, Stephen Valentine, Anthony Ross, Kapr Bangura, Donald Bull, Chris Richardson, Aaron Howard, Sharif Williams, Demetrius Montrose, Marie Bigham, Tamar Adegbile, Kwesi Fraser, André Pinard, Nakia Booth, Kimberly King, Dan Limerick, Duke Amponsah, Susan Tree, Peter Snedecor, Rhonda and Gary Casson, Patty and Michael Chernick, Jill and Paul Aschkenasy, and Dianne Garrett.

For those whose words poured into me then and keep me going now: Gail Karpf, Marysol Castro, Darrick Hamilton, Monique Nelson-Nwachuku, Auntie Irene, Anaya, Primo Khalil, and Mom and Dad. I truly do love you.

To the Wesleyan University Admissions Office in the 1990s. Cliff Thornton, Andy Fairbanks, and Barbara-Jan Wilson, I watched you and learned so much. Thank you.

And to Tim. You used to say "no new friends," and my feelings were hurt. Not anymore. You have been the rock of this project, and I thank you for all that you have brought to the work and to my life. We share a love of Black people and want them to have the information to soar. Thank you for allowing me to be the Robin (or Alfred?) to your Batman. (But I'm 3000!)

In Our Opinion

Shereem

College is not for everyone. Despite what I do for a living and how I am raising my own children, I am not 100 percent convinced that every Black child should go to college, especially not an expensive one that may put them in debt.

From my personal experience as a parent, I am learning that students see college more as an opportunity to have a "good time" than as an educational springboard to adulthood. While this troubles me at times, I am not sure that I viewed college any differently as a teenager. When you're young, you believe you'll always be young, and if you plan on going to college, you may not think about life too far after it. We should encourage our children to have a plan for their lives at age twenty-two and beyond. Because college is such a short window of time in our lives, it should not be the primary destination on the journey of a life well lived.

No matter when we declare ourselves to be an adult, most of us begin learning what we want to learn and how we want to learn it when we're ready. The internet has changed how we educate ourselves, and traditional college may not be right for everyone, although I agree that socializing is not the same without the microcosm of a college campus. We, as parents, should help our children decide what's really important for the marathon of life.

If you want your child to go to college and your child wants to go to college, I want what you want. If you do not want your child to go to college and they do not either, I will not judge you or them, but I will ask you, What's the plan? College gives us the structure and boundaries to formulate a vision for the future. There are resources there that help young people find themselves and get their professional footing. If going to college is what your family has decided to do, you need to educate yourselves on the college options out there and be proactive in finding the right places to visit and ultimately help your child to apply.

College admissions at elite schools—HBCUs and PWIs—can be complicated. Many of us overlook schools that might serve our child better because we believe that a name and a network are critical to success in life. In my opinion, this is true, so if your child is going to go to college, they should have in mind schools with a name and network that will excite them to be on campus and thrive. If, however, your child is an artist, an athlete, or someone intent on finding their own way to success, I hope we can get behind them and applaud their courage. Might they ultimately regret the decision not to attend college? Maybe. Do we all know people we respect and applaud who do not have a college degree? Likely so. The choice is not just between an HBCU and a PWI; the question is, Is college right for my child?

Tim

Throughout this book our goal has been to offer a fair and balanced view on the benefits of both PWIs and HBCUs, but everyone wants to know what we really think. We must have a preference, right? No, we don't, but we have so many opinions. If you had asked me this question—about PWIs versus HBCUs—fifteen to twenty years ago, I would have told you that every Black student, especially Black males, should attend an HBCU, but my personal and professional opinion has evolved over time. For starters, it is not realistic. While there are over a hundred HBCUs across the country, there is simply not enough room at these fine institutions to educate all the Black students who want to go to college. More importantly, Black people are not and have never been monolithic, so the notion that Black students would only want to attend HBCUs does not reflect the reality of all Black families' educational aspirations. If the desire behind wanting all Black students to attend HBCUs is to shield them from this country's racist ills, that is naïve as well. The reality is that Black students need options for their college education, and they need schools that will provide them with the support, resources, and education they need to thrive while in school and succeed in their professional lives.

The decision to go to college is a personal one, and students will be drawn to different things in their college search. The prestige of institutions will drive some, others will lean toward athletic power-houses, and some will be drawn to HBCUs for social and cultural reasons; but the reality is that most will choose a school based on finances, proximity to their family, or other personal circumstances unrelated to the school. Knowing this from my professional experience, I don't prefer HBCUs over PWIs categorically; what I advise, rather, is finding a school that will meet the needs of the family and the student. We all say that it's the student's decision, but the reality is that it's a family decision, and there are any number of circumstances that can influence the choice of a college. I can offer an opinion, of course, but the truth is that I don't know your child, your family, or your situation.

I would love it if every Black male attended Morehouse, but do they want to be in Atlanta? Do they want to attend an all-male school? Does Morehouse have the academic programs they are looking for? And will the school offer the financial aid they need? Is Emory a great institution? Yes. It has been my professional home for the better part of twenty years. But Emory is selective, is a Division III athletic school with no football team, and may not have the diversity a student or family is looking for. I could continue with any number of institutions, and there will be just as many questions given the personal nature of college choice.

What I want is for your family to be candid and open in the college admissions process from beginning to end. If money is a determining factor, explain that to your child up front because that will limit the schools you consider in the college search. If proximity is a priority, factor that in as early as possible. If HBCUs are not an option, ask yourself why. We can talk about the pros and cons of HBCUs versus PWIs. What we can't do, though, is speak to your child's needs, determine what you can afford, or know what is most important to your family in this process.

I do have one very strong opinion about the college admissions process: it should be based on information, and you should make decisions within the walls of your home and not be influenced by those who don't know all that goes into your making this important life decision. If you and your family own this process early, I have no doubt that your child will have an incredible experience at whatever institution your family chooses.

Best Colleges for Black Students

Parents are always asking us, Where should my child apply? We love this question because it allows us to ask about a student's interests, strengths, and aspirations.

Building a college list does not happen in a three-minute conversation off the top of our heads, but we have become familiar with many colleges and universities that we admire and recommend that parents and students research.

Below is a list of schools we've heard praised by parents, educators, and alumni. This list is not data-driven but rather is based on anecdotal evidence. These schools present great academic, social, and cultural opportunities for Black students. Attending one of them can put students on a trajectory toward professional success. The list is fluid and will grow and change with time. We arranged the schools regionally under groups of states. Many of these schools we mentioned earlier in the book, but the list includes additional ones as well. Note that there are many other great schools for Black students we didn't list, but we wanted to provide a starting point.

New York / New Jersey
Adelphi University
Barnard College (women's college)
Binghamton University
Colgate University
Columbia University
Cornell University
Fordham University
Hamilton College
New York University
Princeton University

Purchase College
Rochester Institute of Technology
Rutgers University
Sarah Lawrence College
St. John's University
Syracuse University
University of Rochester
Vassar College

Connecticut / Rhode Island
Brown University
Connecticut College
Trinity College
University of Connecticut
Wesleyan University
Yale University

Massachusetts / New Hampshire / Vermont / Maine
Amherst College
Bates College
Boston College
Boston University
Bowdoin College
Dartmouth College
Harvard University
Massachusetts Institute of Technology
Middlebury College
Mount Holyoke College (women's college)
Northeastern University
Smith College (women's college)
Tufts University
University of Massachusetts at Amherst
Wellesley College (women's college)
Williams College

Pennsylvania
Bryn Mawr College (women's college)
Bucknell University
Carnegie Mellon
Dickinson College
Drexel University
Haverford College
Lehigh University
Swarthmore College
Temple University
University of Pennsylvania
Villanova University

HBCUs
Cheyney University of Pennsylvania
Lincoln University

Delaware/District of Columbia/Maryland/Virginia
American University
College of William and Mary
Georgetown University
George Washington University
James Madison University
Johns Hopkins University
Towson University
Trinity Washington University
University of Maryland–Baltimore County
University of Maryland–College Park
University of Richmond
University of Virginia

HBCUs
Bowie State University
Delaware State University

Hampton University
Howard University
Morgan State University
Norfolk State University
Virginia State University
Virginia Union University

North Carolina/South Carolina
Clemson University
Davidson College
Duke University
Elon University
Queens College
University of North Carolina–Chapel Hill
University of North Carolina–Charlottte
Wake Forest University

HBCUs
Elizabeth City State University
Johnson C. Smith University
North Carolina A&T State University
North Carolina Central University
Shaw University
South Carolina State University
Winston-Salem State University

Georgia/Florida/Tennessee
Agnes Scott College (women's college)
Emory University
Florida State University
Georgia State University
Georgia Tech University
Rhodes College
University of Florida

University of Georgia
University of Miami
University of Tennessee–Knoxville
Vanderbilt University

HBCUs
Clark Atlanta University
Fisk University
Florida A&M University
Fort Valley State University
Morehouse College (men's college)
Savannah State University
Spelman College (women's college)
Tennessee State University

Alabama / Mississippi / Louisiana
Tulane University

HBCUs
Alabama State University
Alcorn State University
Dillard University
Grambling State University
Jackson State University
Southern University and A&M College
Talladega College
Tuskegee University
Xavier University of Louisiana

Arkansas / Oklahoma / Texas
Rice University
Southern Methodist University
Texas Christian University
University of Houston

University of Oklahoma
University of Texas–Arlington
University of Texas–Austin

HBCUs
Langston University
Paul Quinn College
Philander Smith College
Prairie View A&M University
Texas Southern University
University of Arkansas–Pine Bluff
Wiley College

Illinois / Kentucky / Michigan / Ohio / Indiana / Missouri
Berea College
Case Western University
Kenyon College
Northwestern University
Notre Dame University
Oberlin College
University of Chicago
University of Michigan
University of Missouri–Columbia
Washington University in St. Louis

HBCUs
Central State University
Wilberforce University

California / Colorado
California Institute of Technology
Claremont McKenna College
Colorado College
Harvey Mudd College

Occidental College
Pomona College
Scripps College (women's college)
Stanford University
University of California–Berkeley
University of California–Los Angeles
University of Denver
University of Southern California

Frequently Asked Questions

College Search

What do Tim and Shereem think about the Supreme Court's 2023 decision on race-conscious admissions?

We were disappointed, but not surprised, by the elimination of race as a factor to consider in college admissions. We believe it will detrimentally impact Black students' educational opportunities and possibly will impede professional development for some of our young people. We've been here before, however, and we will be resilient. We must continue to fight the racism of educational segregation that aims to deprive young people of access to information that can change their lives for the better.

To be clear, legacy, philanthropic, and athletic admissions preferences, to date, remain intact. This speaks volumes about how some influential members of our government view Black students. Run, dribble, score. This also makes us question why we place so much emphasis on colleges and universities that were never built to educate Black students.

We, along with educational policy makers, will continue to uphold and believe in the importance of diversity in higher education. For our children, though, we must reexamine our intentions and options and, ultimately, redefine success.

What standardized tests should my child take and when?

This is a personal decision, but we would encourage families to explore free test preparation through books or online resources. Students can take a diagnostic test for both the SAT and ACT to see which one would be better to take. Others would encourage students to take both tests to see which one they do better on, and then focus on taking that test again. There is no wrong answer here;

it really depends on what the student is most comfortable with. Ideally, they should not take either test more than three times.

When should test preparation begin?

We recommend starting test prep in the summer after tenth grade. Preparing for the ACT or SAT is not about cramming. Preparation should be gradual because it takes time to learn test-taking strategies and to practice them. Ideally, if a student decides to test, they should have a score they are comfortable with by the beginning of their senior year.

What activities should students do while in high school?

Unless a school asks for specific activities, and most do not, schools simply want to know that a student is authentically interested and productive in an activity outside the classroom. If anything, schools are looking for consistency and commitment to a student's chosen areas of interest.

What if my child has learning differences?

The short answer is **there are no IEPs (Individualized Education Programs) or 504 plans in college.** The Individuals with Disabilities Education Act, the law that provides students with IEPs, no longer applies to them once they graduate from high school. Thus, it's important to contact schools prior to applying to learn about services and accommodations they offer for students with learning differences.

When should we start visiting colleges?

As early as a student's eighth or ninth grade, a family should visit schools any chance they get when they go to see extended family or friends who live near schools of interest. We believe that students should earnestly begin visiting schools as early as the summer following their sophomore year of high school.

Should we be taking virtual tours?

While it's always better to visit a campus in person to get a feel for its culture, the pandemic has pushed schools to increase virtual touring opportunities. Our advice is to try to visit the schools you are most interested in, and for others you may be on the fence about, look into virtual tours.

What should we do when representatives of a college visit our school or area?

Visiting all your schools of interest may be difficult to do. If representatives of a school of interest come to town for a prospective student program, then we encourage the family or student to attend. If the family has already visited that school or taken part in another of its programs, there is no need to attend again, unless the school tracks demonstrated interest.

What is dual enrollment? Should we consider it?

Dual enrollment is when college courses are offered to high school students while they are still in high school. The transfer of these course credits varies by institution, so it's good to have an idea of the schools a student plans to apply to before deciding to take part in dual enrollment. Dual enrollment credits are more likely to transfer to in-state public colleges and universities. If a student wants to apply to some of the more selective schools in the country, they should considerer enrolling in Advanced Placement or International Baccalaureate courses offered at their high school, if they are available, as opposed to enrolling in dual enrollment. What's most important in thinking about dual enrollment is considering whether the courses will be accepted for credit by the institutions the student applies to. Thus, before enrolling in dual enrollment courses, we recommend that the family contact schools of interest and ask them if they accept dual enrollment credits and what is the maximum number of credits an incoming first-year student can bring in. Many private colleges and universities limit the number of dual enrollment credits they accept from those who enroll as first-year students.

Do colleges look at students' social media posts? What kinds of posts are inappropriate?

Students need to know that social media can be used for them or against them. Too often students believe their digital imprint is "private" without realizing that it isn't necessarily. We recommend that students use social media to support their applications, not as public displays meant only for their friends. If a high school student wants to use social media, we would discourage them from posting anything they are not willing to share with the schools they're considering.

College Applications

What is needed for a college application?

The requirements for a college application vary from school to school. Most schools, though, will require the following:

- application form
- essay(s)
- transcript
- tests scores (ACT, SAT, or Advanced Placement scores if applicable; currently many schools are test-optional, so check with individual schools for testing requirements)
- teacher recommendations
- counselor recommendation, or School Report Form

We advise families to visit a school's admissions website to learn about its particular requirements.

How many colleges should my student apply to?

While there is no one-size-fits-all answer, we encourage students to have a balanced college list that includes

- reach schools—those where a student has less than a 25 percent chance of being admitted;
- target schools—those where a student has a 50 percent chance of being admitted; and
- foundational schools—those where a student has a 75 percent chance or better of being admitted.

We think that having three of each (nine schools in total) is a good strategy. *The percentages are based on schools' published admit rates; schools publish ranges for the academic credentials of their last admitted class, and students can compare those ranges with their own credentials to estimate a likelihood of their being admitted.*

What should the college application essay be about?
The college application essay, also known as the personal statement, needs to be honest and revealing. There is no one thing it should be about. Essays should respond to prompts, and leave the reader with takeaways about who the applicant is.

What are supplemental essays? Why are they important?
Supplemental essays are pieces of writing, ranging from 150 words to 650 words, that a school may ask for in addition to the personal statement. The purpose of supplemental essays is usually to see how a candidate thinks, while the personal statement is intended to reveal part of who the candidate is. Supplemental essays are important, oftentimes especially so for smaller college communities.

What are colleges looking for in recommendations? Who should write them?
Recommendation letters are a way for schools to find out additional information about students, specifically related to their intellectual curiosity and character in the classroom. They provide insight into the type of student an applicant would be in college. Given that there's much weight placed on students' academic potential in admissions decisions, teachers are often the best recommender for giving insight into their students' abilities because of the large amount of time they spend with their students. A family can contact a school to find out what categories of recommenders it accepts recommendations from.

When are applications due?
Most schools begin accepting applications on August 1. However, the final deadline is usually October 15, November 1, November 15, December 1, or January 1. Each institution sets its own deadlines,

so they will vary. All students should aim to have their applications submitted in advance of the deadlines.

Are interviews important?

If a college offers an interview—in person, virtual, or with alumni—a student should take advantage of the opportunity. This is a chance for them to ask questions and share who they are and why they are a good match for the school.

What is demonstrated interest?

Demonstrated interest is when institutions consider an applicant's engagement with them during the application process in making their admissions decision. What is considered demonstrated interest varies from school to school, so the best thing to do is ask schools two questions:

(a) Does the school consider demonstrated interest?
(b) What actions count as demonstrated interest?

When should we apply for financial aid?

Each school has its own financial aid deadlines. We recommend that families apply for financial aid in the fall of a student's senior year in high school.

Should we fill out the FAFSA even though we make a lot of money?

Absolutely. How financial aid eligibility is determined varies from school to school. The worst that can happen is a school will turn down a family's application for need-based financial aid. To be eligible for merit aid instead, schools usually need to have the FAFSA and/or CSS Profile on file.

When will we be notified of an admissions decision?

This will depend on what admissions plan an applicant applies under: Early Action, Single-Choice Early Action, Early Decision I, Early Decision II, regular decision, or rolling. Students will have heard from all colleges by early April of their senior year and must make a decision by May 1, which was designated College Signing Day by First Lady Michelle Obama.

College Choice

What should we prioritize in choosing a college?
A family should have an honest conversation about what factors are the most important in determining which college or university is the best choice. The choice may be driven by cost, location, diversity, possible majors, career aspirations, or any number of other reasons. We encourage families to have some kind of a system in place for determining the factors that matter the most.

How do we compare financial aid packages?
Financial aid packages will differ from one institution to the next. Families should look at all aid packages together and consider the bottom-line out-of-pocket expense. The out-of-pocket expense may not be the determining factor in a family's college choice, but we think it's important to consider it. A great resource for comparing financial aid packages is the FinAide app, finaideapp.com.

When does the decision about which college to attend have to be made?
This will vary from school to school, but for many schools in the country, the deadline is May 1. Some schools are willing to grant an extension to accepted applicants who need more time, but such applicants will need to contact the schools before May 1 to make arrangements.

What happens when a student is waitlisted?
A student who's waitlisted is at the mercy of the school as to when they'll hear the school's decision. Each school has its own waitlist procedure, so it's important for waitlisted students to learn about next steps as soon as they receive the waitlisted notification. Even if that school is the student's top choice, we advise the student to begin thinking about other options.

What is a gap year?
A gap year is when a student does not go to college immediately after graduating from high school. There are studies showing that many students are burnt out after thirteen consecutive years of school and

need a year to mature and rejuvenate with a job, travel, or activity. They can then go to college refreshed and ready. We highly recommend that students go ahead and apply to college anyway during their senior year of high school. After being admitted to a college, a student can then pursue the possibility of deferring enrollment for a year.

What is an admissions deposit?

An admissions deposit is usually a nonrefundable deposit that students have to pay to hold their spot in an entering class. The fee varies from school to school, but generally it ranges from one hundred to eight hundred dollars.

Notable Black College Graduates Mentioned in the Book

Person	College/University	Institutional Type	Accomplishments
Kareem Abdul-Jabbar	University of California, Los Angeles	PWI	NBA Player, Author, Actor, Civil Rights Activist
Stacey Abrams	Spelman College	HBCU	Lawyer, Activist, Politician
Eric Adams	John Jay College of Criminal Justice	PWI	Mayor
Byron Allen	University of Southern California	PWI	Comedian, Business Executive
Debbie Allen	Howard University	HBCU	Choreographer, Actor, Producer
Koby Altman	Middlebury College	PWI	Sports Executive
Anthony Anderson	Howard University	HBCU	Actor, Producer
Sydney Barber	United States Naval Academy	PWI	Military Officer
Alicia Boler Davis	Northwestern University	PWI	Business Executive
Julian Bond	Morehouse College	HBCU	Civil Rights Leader
Chadwick Boseman	Howard University	HBCU	Actor
Keisha Lance Bottoms	Florida A&M University	HBCU	Mayor

(continued)

Notable Black College Graduates Mentioned in the Book (*continued*)

Person	College/University	Institutional Type	Accomplishments
Muriel Bowser	Chatham College	PWI	Mayor
Rosalind Brewer	Spelman College	HBCU	Business Executive
Herman Cain	Morehouse College	HBCU	Business Executive
RaaShaun Casey a.k.a. DJ Envy	Hampton University	PWI	Radio Host, Entrepreneur
Kenneth Chenault	Bowdoin College	PWI	Business Executive
Shirley Chisholm	Brooklyn College	PWI	US Representative, Educator, Author
Jim Clyburn	South Carolina State University	HBCU	US Representative
Ryan Coogler	California State University, Sacramento	PWI	Director, Screenwriter
Kizzmekia Corbett	University of Maryland, Baltimore County	PWI	Scientist
Bill Cosby	Temple University	PWI	Actor, Comedian
Tiffany Cross	Clark Atlanta University	HBCU	Journalist
Benjamin Crump	Florida State University	PWI	Civil Rights Lawyer
Stephen Curry	Davidson College	PWI	NBA All-Star, Philanthropist
Nia DaCosta	New York University	PWI	Director, Screenwriter

Person	College/University	Institutional Type	Accomplishments
Morgan DeBaun	Washington University in St. Louis	PWI	Entrepreneur
Thasunda Brown Duckett	University of Houston	PWI	Business Executive
Michael Eric Dyson	Princeton University	PWI	Author, Professor
Kamilah Forbes	Howard University	HBCU	Producer, Filmmaker
Eddie George	Ohio State University	PWI	NFL Player, Head Coach College Football
Glenda Glover	Tennessee State University	HBCU	Higher Education Leader
Victor J. Glover	California Polytechnic State University	PWI	Astronaut
Ed Gordon	Western Michigan University	PWI	Journalist
Amanda Gorman	Harvard College	PWI	National Youth Poet Laureate
Nikole Hannah-Jones	University of Notre Dame	PWI	Author, Activist
Hill Harper	Brown University	PWI	Actor, Activist, Author
Kamala Harris	Howard University	HBCU	US Vice President
Melissa Harris-Perry	Wake Forest University	PWI	Author, Journalist
William Robert Harvey	Hampton University	HBCU	Higher Education Leader
Taraji P. Henson	Howard University	HBCU	Actor

(continued)

Notable Black College Graduates Mentioned in the Book (*continued*)

Person	College/University	Institutional Type	Accomplishments
Jemele Hill	Michigan State University	PWI	Journalist, TV Personality
Mellody Hobson	Princeton University	PWI	Business Executive, NFL Team Co-owner
Langston Hughes	Lincoln University	HBCU	Poet, Social Activist
Zora Neale Hurston	Howard University	HBCU	Author, Anthropologist, Filmmaker
Terrence J	North Carolina A&T State University	HBCU	Actor, TV Host
Hue Jackson	University of the Pacific	PWI	NFL Coach, Head Coach College Football
Rev. Jesse Jackson Sr.	North Carolina A&T State University	HBCU	Civil Rights Activist, Minister
Ketanji Brown Jackson	Harvard College	PWI	Supreme Court Justice
Kerrick Jackson	Bethune-Cookman University & University of Nebraska	HBCU & PWI	Head Coach College Baseball
Samuel L. Jackson	Morehouse College	HBCU	Actor
Erika James	Pomona College	PWI	Higher Education Leader
Robert "Bob" L. Johnson	Princeton University	PWI	Entrepreneur, Media Mogul
Rashida Jones	Hampton University	HBCU	Media Executive
Vernon Jordan	Howard University	HBCU	Business Executive, Civil Rights Attorney

Person	College/University	Institutional Type	Accomplishments
Dr. Martin Luther King Jr.	Morehouse College	HBCU	Civil Rights Leader
Mathew Knowles	Fisk University	HBCU	Business Executive
Malcom D. Lee	Georgetown University	PWI	Screenwriter, Film Director
Spike Lee	Morehouse College	HBCU	Film Director
John Lewis	Fisk University	HBCU	US Representative, Civil Rights Leader
Dan Limerick	Wesleyan University	PWI	Media Executive, Chief Operating Officer
Nicole Lynn	University of Oklahoma	PWI	Sports Agent, Executive
Cynthia Marshall	University of California, Berkeley	PWI	NBA Executive
Thurgood Marshall	Lincoln University	HBCU	US Supreme Court Justice
Roland Martin	Texas A&M University	PWI	Journalist
Tayari McIntosh a.k.a. DJ Trauma	Clark Atlanta University	HBCU	Disc Jockey
Wes Moore	Johns Hopkins University	PWI	Governor, Rhodes Scholar
Toni Morrison	Howard University	HBCU	Poet, Novelist
Edwin Moses	Morehouse College	HBCU	Olympic Gold Medalist
Monique Nelson-Nwachuku	Vanderbilt University	PWI	Business Executive, Philanthropist

(continued)

Notable Black College Graduates Mentioned in the Book (*continued*)

Person	College/University	Institutional Type	Accomplishments
Nyaka NiiLampti	Princeton University	PWI	Sport Psychologist, NFL Executive
Barack Obama	Columbia University	PWI	US President
Michelle Obama	Princeton University	PWI	First Lady, Author, Lawyer
Pam Oliver	Florida A&M University	HBCU	Sports Broadcaster
William Packer	Florida A&M University	HBCU	Film Director, Producer
Vicki Palmer	Rhodes College	PWI	Business Executive
Steve Pamon	Morehouse College	HBCU	Entertainment Executive
Dick Parsons	University of Hawai'i at Mānoa	PWI	Business Executive
Chris Paul	Winston-Salem State University	HBCU	NBA All-Star, HBCU Ambassador
Megan Jovon Ruth Pete a.k.a. Megan Thee Stallion	Texas Southern University	HBCU	Hip-Hop Artist
Billy Porter	Carnegie Mellon University	PWI	Actor, Activist
Phylicia Rashad	Howard University	HBCU	Actor, Director, Singer, Educator
Robi Reed	Hampton University	HBCU	Casting Director, Activist
Steven Reed	Morehouse College	HBCU	Mayor

Person	College/University	Institutional Type	Accomplishments
Joy Reid	Harvard College	PWI	Journalist
Condoleezza Rice	University of Denver	PWI	US Secretary of State, Professor
Jerry Rice	Mississippi Valley State University	HBCU	NFL Player and Hall of Famer
Cedric Richmond	Morehouse College	HBCU	US Representative
Shonda Rhimes	Dartmouth College	PWI	Screenwriter, Producer
Eric Roberson	Howard University	HBCU	Singer, Songwriter
Shaun Robinson	Spelman College	HBCU	Journalist, Media Personality
Tracee Ellis Ross	Brown University	PWI	Actor, Producer
Angela Rye	University of Washington	PWI	Lawyer, Activist
Bozoma "Boz" Saint John	Wesleyan University	PWI	Media Executive
Lisa Salters	Pennsylvania State University	PWI	Journalist, TV Personality
Deion Sanders	Talladega College (Played college football at Florida State University)	HBCU	NFL Player and Hall of Famer, TV Personality, Head Coach College Football
Shannon Sharpe	Savannah State University	HBCU	NFL Player and Hall of Famer, TV Personality
John Singleton	University of Southern California	PWI	Film Director, Screenwriter, Producer, Actor
Robert F. Smith	Cornell University	PWI	Businessman, Philanthropist, Engineer

(continued)

Notable Black College Graduates Mentioned in the Book (*continued*)

Person	College/University	Institutional Type	Accomplishments
Stephen A. Smith	Winston-Salem State University	HBCU	Sports Journalist, TV Personality
Michael Sorrell	Oberlin College	PWI	Higher Education Leader
Dawn Staley	University of Virginia	PWI	Olympic Champion, WNBA Player, Head Coach College Basketball
David Steward	University of Central Missouri	PWI	Business Executive
Michael Strahan	Texas Southern University	HBCU	NFL Player, TV Personality
Beverly Daniel Tatum	Wesleyan University	PWI	Psychologist, Author, Educator
Clarence Thomas	College of the Holy Cross	PWI	Supreme Court Justice
Rebecca Walker	Yale University	PWI	Author, Activist
Tristan Walker	State University of New York at Stony Brook	PWI	Entrepreneur
Raphael Warnock	Morehouse College	HBCU	US Senator, Minister
Kerry Washington	George Washington University	PWI	Actor, Activist
Maxine Waters	California State University, Los Angeles	PWI	US Representative
Susan Kelechi Watson	Howard University	HBCU	Actress

Person	College/University	Institutional Type	Accomplishments
Fawn Weaver	University of Alabama	PWI	Founder and CEO of Uncle Nearest Premium Whiskey
Cornel West	Princeton University	PWI	Professor, Presidential Candidate
Michael Wilbon	Northwestern University	PWI	Journalist, TV Personality
Oprah Winfrey	Tennessee State University	HBCU	Media Mogul, Philanthropist
Randall Woodfin	Morehouse College	HBCU	Mayor
Roy Woods Jr.	Florida A&M University	HBCU	Comedian
Jason Wright	Northwestern University	PWI	NFL Executive
Angela Yee	Wesleyan University	PWI	Radio Host
Andrew Young	Howard University	HBCU	Mayor, Ambassador, Civil Rights Leader

Suggested Reading

Akerele, Zakiya. *Dump Your Degree: How to Repurpose Your Education, Control Your Career, and Gain Financial Freedom* (2021).

Barnard, Brennan, and Rick Clark. *The Truth about College Admission: A Family Guide to Getting In and Staying Together*, 2nd ed. (2023).

Bowen, William G., and Derek Bok. *The Shape of the River: Long-Term Consequences of Considering Race in College and University Admissions* (1998).

Bruni, Frank. *Where You Go Is Not Who You'll Be: An Antidote to the College Admissions Mania* (2016).

Cary, Lorene. *Black Ice* (1991).

Cole, J. *Get 'em Out: Help Your Teen Discover a Successful Path to College (. . . and Out of Your House)* (2019).

Deresiewicz, William. *Excellent Sheep: The Miseducation of the American Elite and the Way to a Meaningful Life* (2014).

DiAngelo, Robin. *White Fragility: Why It's So Hard for White People to Talk about Racism* (2018).

Dyson, Michael Eric. *Entertaining Race: Performing Blackness in America* (2021).

Espy, Stephanie. *STEM Gems: How 44 Women Shine in Science, Technology, Engineering and Mathematics, and How You Can Too!* (2016).

Freeman, Kassie. *African Americans and College Choice: The Influence of Family and School* (2005).

Furda, Eric J., and Jacques Steinberg. *The College Conversation: A Practical Companion for Parents to Guide Their Children along the Path to Higher Education* (2020).

Graham, Lawrence Otis. *Our Kind of People: Inside America's Black Upper Class* (1999).

Green, Khalid Diallo Akhdaru. *Free Game: A Parents' Guide to Navigating Black/Brown Children through Youth Sports and Beyond* (2023).

Hamblet, Elizabeth C. *Seven Steps to College Success: A Pathway for Students with Disabilities*, 3rd ed. (2023).

Heffernan, Lisa, and Mary Dell Harrington. *Grown and Flown: How to Support Your Teen, Stay Close as a Family, and Raise Independent Adults* (2019).

Horn, Michael B., and Bob Moesta. *Choosing College: How to Make Better Learning Decisions throughout Your Life* (2019).

Jack, Anthony Abraham. *The Privileged Poor: How Elite Colleges Are Failing Disadvantaged Students* (2019).

Lemann, Nicholas. *The Big Test: The Secret History of the American Meritocracy* (1999).

Lieber, Ron. *The Price You Pay for College: An Entirely New Road Map for the Biggest Financial Decision Your Family Will Ever Make* (2021).

Lovett, Bobby L. *America's Historically Black Colleges and Universities: A Narrative History, 1837–2009* (2015).

Mamlet, Robin, and Christine Vandevelde. *College Admission: From Application to Acceptance, Step by Step* (2011).

Marcus, David L. *Acceptance: A Legendary Guidance Counselor Helps Seven Kids Find the Right Colleges—and Find Themselves* (2009).

Mitchell, Josh. *The Debt Trap: How Student Loans Became a National Catastrophe* (2021).

Obama, Michelle. *Becoming* (2018).

ONeal, Anthony. *The Debt Free Degree: The Step-by-Step Guide to Getting Your Kid through College without Student Loans* (2019).

Pope, Loren. *Colleges That Change Lives: 40 Schools That Will Change the Way You Think about Colleges* (2006).

Reddick, Richard J. *Restorative Resistance in Higher Education: Leading in an Era of Racial Awakening and Reckoning* (2023).

Sabky, Becky Munsterer. *Valedictorians at the Gate: Standing Out, Getting In, and Staying Sane While Applying to College* (2021).

Scott, Carjie. *You Are Accepted: How to Get Accepted into College and Life* (2021).

Selingo, Jeffrey. *Who Gets In and Why: A Year inside College Admissions* (2020).

Steinberg, Jacques. *The Gatekeepers: Inside the Admissions Process of a Premier College* (2002).

Tanabe, Gen, and Kelly Tanabe. *The Ultimate Scholarship Book, 2022: Billions of Dollars in Scholarships, Grants and Prizes* (2021).

Tatum, Beverly Daniel. *Why Are All the Black Kids Sitting Together in the Cafeteria? And Other Conversations about Race* (1997).

Tough, Paul. *The Inequality Machine: How College Divides Us* (2021).

————. *The Years That Matter Most: How College Makes or Breaks Us* (2019).

Walker, Sheryl. *The Black Girl's Guide to College Success: What No One Really Tells You about College That You Must Know* (2007).

Wilkerson, Isabel. *Caste: The Origins of Our Discontents* (2020).

Zasloff, Beth, and Joshua Steckel. *Hold Fast to Dreams: A College Guidance Counselor, His Students, and the Vision of a Life beyond Poverty* (2015).

Glossary

accreditation. The recognition by an outside agency that a school maintains certain curricular standards. Having a degree from an accredited institution lets students qualify for admission to other accredited institutions.

ACT (American College Test). A standardized test that is often required for admission to college. The test is divided into four sections: English, Math, Reading, and Science.

admissions requirements. A set of rules established by every college or university for determining whether students qualify for admission.

Advanced Placement (AP). Advanced high school classes that allow students to earn credit that can be transferred to a college and may let them bypass entry-level college courses. Credit is earned only if a student earns a high enough score on a standardized test. Most highly selective schools expect applicants to have taken AP courses in high school.

AP Scholar. An award recognizing high school students who have shown college-level achievement through their performance on multiple AP tests. There are several levels to the award.

associate's degree. An associate's degree is earned after completing a program of study at a two-year college, typically a community or junior college. The degree is usually an associate of arts or an associate of science.

audit. When a student attends a class for the purpose of gaining information without completing all assignments or taking all tests. No grade or credit is given.

bachelor's degree. A degree awarded for completing a college academic program of at least four years. These degrees are usually a bachelor of arts (BA) or a bachelor of science (BS).

CEEB Code (College Entrance Examination Board Code). A unique identification number assigned to each high school and college. This code appears on the high school profile or can be obtained from a school counselor or searched for online.

College Board. A nonprofit organization that provides tests and other educational services for students, high schools, and colleges. The SAT (Scholastic Assessment Test), College Scholarship Search Profile, and AP tests are products of the College Board.

College Scholarship Search Profile (CSS Profile). A financial aid form used by many private colleges to award private, non-federal funds.

Common Application. The Common Application is an undergraduate college admissions application that applicants may use to apply to more than nine hundred member colleges and universities in all fifty states and the District of Columbia and in Canada, China, Japan, and many European countries.

cost of attendance. The total cost of college for one year as a full-time student. This covers the cost of tuition, room and board, books, transportation, and personal expenses.

credit. Credits, also known as "semester hours," are earned when students successfully complete a college class. A full-time college student is usually defined as someone who attends three to four classes a term and earns at least twelve credits per term.

CSS Profile. *See* College Scholarship Search Profile (CSS Profile).

cumulative record. The complete record of all courses and grades earned by a student. A student's transcript is a copy of their cumulative record.

defer. For students who apply Early Decision or Early Action, a school may decide not to admit or deny them at first but may defer making a decision and reevaluate the applicant among the general pool of applicants.

degree. A certificate indicating satisfactory completion of a program of study. A four-year degree is typically a BA (bachelor of arts) or a BS (bachelor of science). A graduate degree beyond a bachelor's may be an MA (master of arts) or an MS (master of science). There are also a law degree (JD, or doctor of jurisprudence), a medical degree (MD, or doctor of medicine), a PhD (doctor of philosophy), and many others.

Early Action. A nonbinding admissions plan whereby students apply in October or November and receive a decision within thirty to ninety days.

Early Decision. A binding admissions plan in which the student, parents, and counselor all agree, in writing, that if the student is admitted, they will attend. Deadlines are typically in November for Early Decision I and January for Early Decision II. With both plans, students receive a decision within approximately six weeks.

FAFSA (Free Application for Federal Student Aid). Completing this form allows applicants to apply for financial aid in the form of scholarships, grants, loans, and work-study.

Federal Direct Loan. Formerly known as a Stafford Loan, this is a loan from the US government for student financial aid.

fee waiver. Students who register to take a standardized test or who submit an application to a college can apply to be relieved of having to pay the associated fee. This request is often granted when a family's income falls below a certain threshold.

financial aid. Scholarships, grants, loans, and work-study programs allow students to attend college when their families demonstrate a need for additional money to pay for college. Financial aid packages are determined by a family's financial need as measured by their assets, liabilities, and debt-to-income ratio. Some financial aid is also determined by the availability of government funds.

grade point average (GPA). The total number of grade points earned divided by the number of credits taken.

grant. Financial aid that does not need to be repaid. It is usually awarded based on need or academic achievement or a special skill, talent, or heritage.

International Baccalaureate. A course of study that allows high school students to satisfy the curricular admissions requirements of universities in more than seventy countries.

liberal arts college. A college where the emphasis of the curricula is on philosophy, literature, history, languages, and basic science.

major. A student's primary field of study.

master's degree. The degree given for completing a one- to two-year course of study beyond a bachelor's degree. Some examples: master of arts (MA), master of science (MS), master of business administration (MBA), and master of fine arts (MFA).

minor. A subject-area emphasis earned by completing a certain number of credits in an area outside a student's major.

part-time student. A college student who takes fewer than a full-time schedule of classes (usually twelve to sixteen units, or credit hours, per term); part-time status may make students ineligible for financial aid.

Pell Grant. Financial aid from the federal government available to students with significant financial need at many types of colleges and vocational schools.

prerequisite. Courses, test scores, and/or grade level that must be completed or attained before a student is permitted to enroll in a particular course.

private college. A college that is not supported by state taxes.

provisional acceptance. Acceptance to a college that pends submission of a final GPA, proof of graduation, or some other documentation of a student's scholastic record.

PSAT/NMSQT (Preliminary Scholastic Aptitude Test / National Merit Scholarship Qualifying Test). A shortened version of the SAT offered in October to high school juniors and younger. The scores offer an initial assessment for college planning and may help students qualify for National Merit Scholarships.

REA (Restrictive Early Action) / SCEA (Single-Choice Early Action). Offered by several elite colleges such as Harvard, Princeton, and Yale, REA allows students to receive an admissions decision early with a nonbinding application. When students apply REA, they cannot also apply Early Decision at other schools.

regular decision. The standard admissions plan with application deadlines usually between January 1 and March 30.

rolling admissions. The ongoing review of applications without a formal deadline. The earlier a student applies, the earlier they will be notified of a decision. Colleges accept as many students as they need to fill an incoming class.

ROTC (Reserve Officers Training Corps). Many colleges have ROTC programs that offer years of military training culminating in an officer's commission. At some colleges, credits for ROTC courses can be applied toward a degree. ROTC scholarships, which pay for full college costs, are available.

SAT (Scholastic Assessment Test). A college admissions exam measuring critical reading and math reasoning skills.

scholarship. A gift of money (which does not need to be repaid) given in recognition of student financial need or achievement, skills, or talent.

school profile. This document, produced by high schools, provides school demographic information, curriculum, GPA and class rank calculation, extracurricular activities offered, and other information about the school to give admissions offices an understanding of what was available to an applicant in high school.

Student Aid Index (SAI). The amount of financial aid that federal formulas determine a student is eligible to receive in a given year. Formerly, this calculation was called the expected family contribution, or EFC.

Student Aid Report. A form distributed by the College Scholarship Service for the purpose of estimating the family contribution to a student's college costs.

superscoring. Taking SAT or ACT subscores from different test administrations to assemble the highest combined score.

test-blind. Institutions that do not factor standardized test scores in their admissions decisions even if applicants submit them are said to be test-blind.

test-optional. Institutions that do not require standardized test scores for admissions are said to be test-optional. These institutions will, however, review scores from applicants who opt to submit them.

transcript. An official copy of a student's high school or college courses taken and the grades they earned.

transfer courses. College courses that may be transferred to another college.

tuition. The fee for instruction at a college or vocational school.

waitlist. Colleges admit, reject, or waitlist applicants. Depending on how many admitted students accept the offer to attend, colleges can admit students from the waiting list.

weighted course. An admissions policy applied to high school students' GPAs that rewards difficult classes taken.

work-study. A federally funded program that makes part-time jobs available to students with demonstrated financial need.

Index

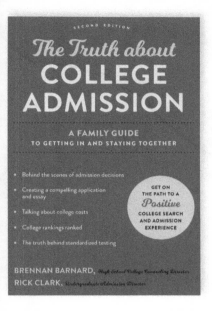
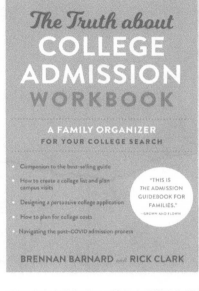
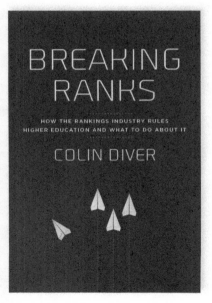
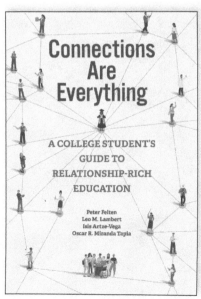